PRESENTED TO:

_____

PET'S NAME

_____

OWNER'S NAME

_____

DATE

Paws in His Presence

Paws in His Presence

50 Inspirational Animal Stories to Help You
Pray & Ponder the Psalms

JENNIFER MARSHALL BLEAKLEY

TYNDALE
MOMENTUM®

A Tyndale nonfiction imprint

Visit Tyndale online at tyndale.com.

Visit Tyndale Momentum online at tyndalemomentum.com.

Tyndale, Tyndale's quill logo, *Tyndale Momentum*, and the Tyndale Momentum logo are registered trademarks of Tyndale House Ministries. Tyndale Momentum is a nonfiction imprint of Tyndale House Publishers, Carol Stream, Illinois.

Paws in His Presence: 50 Inspirational Animal Stories to Help You Pray and Ponder the Psalms

Designed by Eva M. Winters

Edited by Bonne Steffen

Published in association with the literary agency, WTA Media LLC, Franklin, TN.

Unless otherwise indicated, all Scripture quotations are taken from the *Holy Bible,* New Living Translation, copyright © 1996, 2004, 2015 by Tyndale House Foundation. Used by permission of Tyndale House Publishers, Carol Stream, Illinois 60188. All rights reserved. Scripture quotations marked GNT are taken from the Good News Translation in Today's English Version, Second Edition, copyright © 1992 by American Bible Society. Used by permission. Scripture quotations marked ICB are taken from the International Children's Bible®. Copyright © 1986, 1988, 1999 by Thomas Nelson. Used by permission. All rights reserved. Scripture quotations marked NIV are taken from the Holy Bible, *New International Version,*® *NIV.*® Copyright © 1973, 1978, 1984, 2011 by Biblica, Inc.® Used by permission. All rights reserved worldwide.

For information about special discounts for bulk purchases, please contact Tyndale House Publishers at csresponse@tyndale.com, or call 1-855-277-9400.

ISBN 978-1-4964-8771-1

Printed in China

30	29	28	27	26	25	24
7	6	5	4	3	2	1

For Brooklyn and PD

and all the animals at Arise—

thank you for being a safe place for so many.

Introduction

I WISH I COULD TELL YOU that the idea for this book bubbled up from my joy-filled heart as I was frolicking with puppies and kittens in a field of wildflowers—which, just so you know, is how I wish all book ideas would begin! But the truth is, the idea for this book came in the midst of one of the most painful seasons of life I've ever walked through. In fact, this book started less as an idea and more as a desperate plea for help.

A plea for God to intervene in a situation; to fix what was broken; to heal things in such a dramatic way that everyone who saw it would be amazed. I wanted a burning bush. I wanted to escape a fiery furnace. I wanted him to part the seas of my fear, doubt, and pain.

I wanted a mountaintop miracle, ushered in by holy thunder and a choir of heavenly hosts.

I wanted God to wow me with his actions.

Instead, he rescued me with his presence.

And he did so through the Psalms and animals.

While I was begging God for a dramatic answer to my prayers, he was gently leading my heart to the Psalms—a book I often turn to when life gets hard and my emotions swirl. But this time as I read the collection of prayers, praises, and laments, I did so with animals around me.

With Gracie, my Golden retriever, resting her head in my lap.

With my Maine coon cat, Foxy, pawing at my hand as I journaled.

With birds eating their fill at the feeders on the deck and squirrels scampering up and down the pine trees when I sat outside to pray.

And on more than one occasion, with horses listening and barn cats purring, while I walked around a friend's horse ranch pondering a particular psalm.

Over and over again, in the midst of my darkness and despair, my heart would be buoyed—not by God making everything right, but by experiencing his presence through the Psalms and the animals that were with me. As I read the God-breathed, God-inspired words, the animals around me became a living, breathing picture of God's presence with me.

God wove the words with the tangible presence of his animal ambassadors to create a lifeline for my weary heart.

A lifeline I want to share with you.

I can't tell you that everything is going to work out the way you long for it to. I can't fix what is broken. I can't promise you that your hard season is almost over.

But I can tell you that you are not alone.

I can tell you that you are loved—and your loved ones are loved—more than you can fathom.

And I can promise you that because God is with you, you will get through this. Whatever you are facing, whatever is breaking your heart, whatever has you paralyzed with fear is no match for God's presence with you.

God Almighty, the Creator and King of the universe is with you—right now, in this moment.

The great I Am is with you, even in this. And he will sustain you.

This book is proof.

Because he was with me in the midst of my darkest hour.

As I said, I wanted him to wow me with his actions; but instead he rescued me with his presence. By being there. And he can do the same for you.

As you read this book, I pray that you will experience God in a new and powerful way.

Each story opens with a passage from Psalms. I encourage you to read the verses aloud, if possible. Linger over the words. Ask God to meet you in them— he is there.

Each Scripture portion is followed by a true story involving an animal. Some are amusing; some are heartwarming; a few are heartbreaking. Some are my personal stories; some are stories from friends; some are stories from strangers who have become friends. All of them invite you to see yourself, or a loved one, in the story.

After you read the story, take a few minutes to ponder what you've read by answering some reflection questions. These are especially helpful to do with a pet or friend nearby. As you think about the questions, ask God to speak to your soul and remind your heart that he is with you.

One practice that has been so incredibly helpful to me has been learning to pray the Psalms. Taking the words God recorded for us and speaking them back to him has breathed new life into my prayer time. So after the ponder section, you will find the Psalm passage rewritten as a prayer. Feel free to pray the words as they are written or write your own prayer from the passage. This practice alone has helped me in so many ways.

Each story also includes a takeaway statement that summarizes the passage and story, a little nugget of truth that you could write down or ponder throughout the day.

Writing this book felt like both an act of worship and an act of healing.

I pray your heart receives it as both. I pray you will encounter the healing, sustaining, rescuing, loving, and redeeming presence of God as you engage with this book.

Now, I invite you to take a deep breath.

Think of your favorite animal.

And prepare to paws in God's presence . . .

With you on this journey,

Much love,

Jen

The God Who Offers Rest

Yes, my soul, find rest in God;
my hope comes from him.
Truly he is my rock and my salvation;
he is my fortress, I will not be shaken.
My salvation and my honor depend on God;
he is my mighty rock, my refuge.
Trust in him at all times, you people;
pour out your hearts to him,
for God is our refuge.

PSALM 62:5-8, NIV

Paws

"Sorry, Oscar, my meeting ran late," Bryan said rushing into the house.

Grabbing a red leash from a hook by the door, he clipped it to his basset hound's collar.

Ten-year-old Oscar barely made it to the grassy area outside of Bryan's town house before lifting his leg. A pang of guilt hit Bryan's heart. His new promotion had certainly increased his bank account—and his blood pressure—but it had significantly decreased his downtime, especially time with Oscar. Yet with so many layoffs happening at his company, he felt like he had to prove himself or all he'd have would be downtime.

Oscar's ears brushed the ground as he tracked a scent. Bryan glanced at his watch. *Twenty-eight minutes till my next call.*

"Come on, little buddy. Let's take a quick walk around the lake like we used to."

Oscar's long brown ears flopped as he ran to catch up to Bryan. He pranced with the excitement of a puppy as they began their walk around the small lake in the center of their town house complex. But soon his pace slowed. Oscar lowered his head to sniff the grass. He sniffed a nearby bush, then a ball of moss. He stopped to scratch the back of his ear. He looked up at Bryan and then sat down on the sidewalk.

"Come on, Oscar," Bryan said, giving the leash a gentle tug. He checked his watch. *Fifteen minutes.* "We gotta pick up the pace, buddy. I'm presenting in this meeting."

Oscar looked up at Bryan and released a long sigh.

Bryan tugged a little firmer on the leash. "Oscar, let's go."

But Oscar didn't budge. Familiar fears rolled through Bryan's mind:

You have to present perfectly, or they will fire you.

If your project fails, you will be the next to go.

If you don't give this job everything you have, you will have nothing.

His chest tightened. Ever since his company announced the first round of layoffs eighteen months ago, he had been working seventy-hour weeks to try to prove his value, his worth.

"I'll dial it back once I reach this goal," he would say to himself.

"I'll take a vacation as soon as I meet this deadline," he would justify.

"I'll be able to rest once I know my job is secure," he would rationalize.

But the goals, deadlines, and metrics kept moving.

As Bryan's mental spiral continued, Oscar lowered his round belly to the sidewalk and laid his brown-and-white head between his front paws. The dog released another sigh. Bryan's affection for his faithful companion filled his heart, and he conceded to his aging dog's not-so-subtle request to rest.

Eight minutes. A pang of fear darted through Bryan's mind, but he refused to let it land. Instead, he sat down beside Oscar and stroked his dog's long silky ears. As he paid attention to Oscar under the shade of a sprawling oak tree, he also noticed the breeze on his face. He heard birds singing overhead. He smelled the sweet scent of gardenias. He watched a ladybug walk across a leaf. And he remembered the God who made it all—and holds it all together.

Bryan inhaled deeply and exhaled fully. For the first time in many weeks, his mind grew quiet. His body grew still, and he rested beside the dog who had been with him through so much.

Then he sent a text to his team letting them know he would be a little late for the meeting. His job was important, but sitting there beside Oscar, he realized that rest—and trust—are important too.

Ponder

What kind of rest is described in the first two lines of this psalm? How does soul rest differ from physical rest? God is described as a rock in this passage. What does that mean? What have you been turning to for rest lately? How might you encourage and remind your soul to rest in God today?

PRAY

God, you are where my soul finds rest. You are my hope, my rock, and my salvation. You are the fortress I can run to, my safe place that can never be shaken. God, teach my soul to rest in the grace of your salvation and in the awareness that my worth, value, and honor are found in you—and in you alone. Keep me grounded in you—my rock and my refuge. Hold my heart close to you, and help me trust in you at all times. I give you my fears and anxieties, my struggles and hopes, my plans and my dreams. I know that they all are safe with you.

Paws in His Presence

God will provide rest for my soul.

The God Who Gives

You, LORD, are all I have,
and you give me all I need;
my future is in your hands.
How wonderful are your gifts to me;
how good they are!
I praise the LORD, because he guides me,
and in the night my conscience warns me.
I am always aware of the LORD's presence;
he is near, and nothing can shake me. . . .
You will show me the path that leads to life;
your presence fills me with joy
and brings me pleasure forever.

PSALM 16:5-8, 11, GNT

Paws

A black cat cowered among a stack of boxes in Lynn's garage one morning. The pupils in the tiny kitten's fear-filled green eyes were mere slits.

"Where did you come from, little one?"

Stray cats were a common sight in the wooded land around her property, but one had never made its way into her garage before this. It was clear that the kitten, who couldn't have been more than a few months old, needed help.

Thankfully, the small creature had wandered into the right garage. Having rescued countless cats over the years, Lynn knew just what to do—beginning with getting the terrified little kitten into a cat carrier so she had a safe place to rest until she was examined by a veterinarian. At the appointment, the vet confirmed the kitten was severely malnourished and needed to be treated for worms.

Armed with prescription food and medication, Lynn took the cat she named Wednesday—for the day of the week she discovered her—back home and set up a cat-friendly zone for her in the guest bathroom. She would give the kitten time to heal and gain strength before allowing her to roam free in the house where Lynn's two very active hound-mix dogs liked to roughhouse and play.

Over time, Wednesday went from skittish to sociable and was soon seeking Lynn out to play and receive pets and scratches. In fact, Wednesday became so social that several months after finding her, Lynn thought about taking her to the barn at the edge of her property where she could play with the three other cats she had rescued a year earlier. However, Lynn worried the three older, much larger cats might scare Wednesday—or take advantage of her petite size.

"Maybe you'd better stay here with me instead," Lynn told the affectionate little cat.

However, three months later, when Lynn heard about another stray cat in need of a home, she knew just what to do. After giving the orange stray, whom she named Garfield, time to adjust to herself and to Wednesday, she took the pair down to the barn. The other barn cats were a little wary of the newcomers. But Lynn gave them all time to adjust by keeping Wednesday and Garfield in a large empty stall in the chicken coop for several days. The cats got to know each other through the chicken wire, and when Lynn finally opened the door it seemed as if the five cats had always been together. They played together, explored the woods together, and napped in the hayloft together.

Life would have been perfect for Wednesday, except for one problem—her little legs were too short to climb down from the hayloft. While the four bigger cats could easily navigate the attached ladder to come and go at will, Wednesday could only climb up. When her feline friends scampered down, she would cry from the loft.

As soon as Lynn figured out what was happening, she moved a tall plastic cabinet next to the ladder and created stairs with hay bales and bags of cedar bedding. She had to physically set Wednesday on the cabinet the first time, but the little black cat quickly caught on and now she is often the first one down from the hayloft. Wednesday isn't the least bit concerned about her size any longer because she knows Lynn watches out for her.

Ponder

Do you find comfort in knowing your future is in God's hands? Why or why not? What are some of the gifts God has given you? How does God guide his children? Can you recall a time he guided you? Take a moment to ponder God's presence. Focus your mind on his nearness. As you inhale and exhale, repeat this truth: *God is here.*

PRAY

Lord, you are all I have, and you give me all I need; my future is in your hands. How wonderful are your gifts to me; how good they are. You guide and direct me. You are always with me. Help me become more aware of your presence. Remind my heart that I don't need to be afraid because you are with me. Show me the path that leads to life and fill my heart with everlasting joy.

--- Paws in His Presence ---

I can trust God to provide what I need.

The God Who Equips

I have chosen to be faithful;
I have determined to live by your regulations.
I cling to your laws.
LORD, don't let me be put to shame!
I will pursue your commands,
for you expand my understanding.
Teach me your decrees, O LORD;
I will keep them to the end.
Give me understanding and I will obey your instructions;
I will put them into practice with all my heart.

PSALM 119:30-34

Paws

Trish couldn't remember a time in her life that she didn't love God and know she was loved by him. She had placed her faith and trust in Jesus when she was six, sitting on her Strawberry Shortcake comforter and praying with her dad. Trish had grown in her knowledge and understanding of the gospel and matured in her faith over the years, but she always treasured that moment when she became a true child of God. And since that day Trish had made every effort to follow his will for her life.

It wasn't always linear, and it had been far from perfect, but Trish had always tried to live out the words of the chorus to her favorite childhood hymn, "Trust and Obey." She would study the Bible, spend time in prayer, regularly attend church, and give of her time, talents, and money to serve and bless others. But there was one command in Scripture she found incredibly difficult to obey—sharing her faith with others.

As an introvert who avoided confrontation like it was her full-time job, the idea of boldly sharing her faith with others felt impossible. She wanted others to know the hope she had, and she wanted to obey Jesus' parting words to his followers to go and make disciples of all nations. But every time she would try to talk to someone about her faith her heart would pound, her hands would tingle, and her throat would feel like she'd swallowed a handful of cotton balls.

"God, I want to share your love with others," she would pray while petting her labradoodle, Freddie, "but I don't know how. If you want me to share, please make a way."

Years passed without a miraculous dose of courage transforming her into a bold witness. Trish began to accept that God gives different gifts to his children. *Maybe my role is to support people who do boldly share the gospel.* So she donated money, prayed for missionaries, and packed boxes of food and supplies for organizations that worked to meet the physical and spiritual needs of others.

One morning at church, she noticed a woman standing beside a small dog. The dog was wearing a green vest with the words PET ME! I'M A THERAPY DOG.

Trish walked over and learned that the woman was part of a new ministry that took therapy dogs to hospitals, college campuses, nursing homes, schools—anywhere people could use a little hope. "The ministry is mainly about the dogs," the woman named Helen said, "but the dogs often open the door to spiritual conversations, and many times we end up sharing our faith and praying for people."

The woman's face was beaming as she talked about the ministry. Her passion ignited Trish's own, and a few weeks later, Trish was getting Freddie certified as a therapy dog and joining the ministry. She was nervous about going on her first visit with Freddie, but since she would be with several other volunteer teams at the college campus, she wasn't too concerned. Besides, Freddie was as extroverted as Trish was introverted.

"You just be you, and we will be fine," Trish told her dog as she straightened his vest.

Within minutes, two dozen college students surrounded the dogs. Most of them were smiling as they rubbed the dogs' bellies and shook their paws, but Trish noticed one young woman standing off to the side. She was close enough to be considered part of the group, but far enough away that Trish suspected the young woman felt miles distant.

"Freddie, let's go say hi," Trish spoke softly to her dog, leading him to the young woman.

"Is it okay if my dog, Freddie, says hi?" she asked.

The young woman nodded and knelt down to pet Freddie.

"He looks like my dog, Bean," she said.

"It must be hard to be away from Bean."

"It's so hard," the girl admitted, her eyes revealing just how much she missed him.

Trish began to talk to the young woman—whose name she learned was Ana—about how lonely she had felt at college and how difficult it had been to make friends. "I finally found a group of friends my junior year," Trish said, smiling at the memory. "We had the same major and started studying together. They helped me so much."

Then without thinking, Trish added, "I'll start praying that you find a group of friends, Ana." The moment the words left her mouth she worried she might have offended the college student. But instead, Ana's eyes filled with tears, and she whispered, "Thank you."

Two weeks later, Trish and Freddie went back to the campus and were delighted when Ana walked up. "I made a friend," she said, her eyes focused on Freddie and a beautiful smile on her lips. "Thanks for praying for me. Um . . . do you really think God cares about me making a friend?"

Trish couldn't believe she was standing on a college campus talking to a young woman about prayer and faith and the hope she had in Jesus. And that was exactly what she did for the next hour, and faithfully every other week for the next four years, visiting with Ana and many other students—with Freddie by her side each and every visit.

Ponder

Have you put your faith and trust in Jesus? Was there a specific moment in time or more of a gradual awareness and surrender? Do you find it difficult to share your faith with others? How have you chosen to be faithful to God? Which of God's commands do you struggle most with? Which come easiest to you? Where are you lacking understanding today? Will you take a few minutes and talk to God about that?

Lord, help me be faithful to you and your will. Grant me the strength and desire to live by your commands and according to the way that you say is best. Help me hold fast to your Word and not walk away from you. Please give me resolve to pursue righteousness for I know that your way is life. Expand my understanding. Teach me your ways and help me keep them. Please grant me wisdom and understanding, and let me live for you all my days.

Paws in His Presence

God equips me to live for him.

The God of Mercy

Answer me when I call to you,
my righteous God.
Give me relief from my distress;
have mercy on me and hear my prayer.
How long will you people turn my glory into shame?
How long will you love delusions and seek false gods?
Know that the LORD has set apart his faithful servant for himself;
the LORD hears when I call to him.
Tremble and do not sin;
when you are on your beds,
search your hearts and be silent. . . .
In peace I will lie down and sleep,
for you alone, LORD,
make me dwell in safety.

PSALM 4:1-4, 8, NIV

Paws

Seven horses grazed peacefully in a large field, nibbling blades of grass, munching on stalks of hay. A gentle breeze rustled the tops of nearby trees, and a flock of geese honked greetings from above. The scene defined serene, yet John noticed none of it. His gaze was on his mud-covered boots as his hands balled into tight fists. His thoughts raced, and he became filled with dread.

The only reason he had agreed to attend the veterans' program at the equine therapy ranch was because he couldn't take his wife's tears anymore. She had begged him to see a counselor—a doctor, a pastor, anyone who might be able to help him. John tried to humor her, but he knew the truth. He had seen too much. Done too much. There was no help for someone like him.

But when she brought home a flyer about a program at a nearby horse ranch for veterans dealing with post-traumatic stress symptoms and begged him to

19

attend, John knew he owed it to her to give it a try. But now that he had arrived, all he wanted to do was run.

John's head jerked up at the sound of a car door slamming. His breath came in shallow pants. He was just about to bolt when a petite woman with wheat-colored hair and a warm smile invited him into the pasture.

"Hi, there," she said, opening a nearby gate. "I'm Jodi, and I'm so glad you're here. Would you like to come meet some of our horses?"

He didn't, but he didn't want to be rude. John steeled himself for what he assumed would be her pitch to try to sell him on the program, convince him to make a donation, or guilt him into therapy.

Instead, she handed him a round brush with short bristles and asked if he had any experience with horses.

"Not really," he admitted.

A brown-and-white horse walked up and bumped Jodi's shoulder with its nose.

"This is Cody," she said, demonstrating the proper way to brush a horse. "He's always up for an adventure."

John's heart rate sped up. He started to sweat.

Not now, he commanded his body—not that his body ever listened.

He definitely didn't want to expose the nice woman to one of his wretched panic attacks, so John scanned the area for an escape route. Something bumped him from behind. He jumped.

"Oh, that's just Mercy," Jodi said. "She wants to say hello."

John's focus moved to the black horse. Their eyes met, and John felt an unfamiliar sense of calm wash over him.

Grateful for the unexpected reprieve, he began brushing the horse like Jodi had shown him. It was strangely soothing. Jodi told John a little bit of Mercy's background—she had been rescued from a horribly abusive situation and had to slowly learn to trust people again.

His heart went out to the horse, and a protectiveness he didn't expect welled up inside him.

Jodi left the two alone and went to speak with some other veterans. John continued to move the brush in small circles. And as he did, his mind grew blissfully quiet.

He exhaled.

Mercy exhaled.

That night John slept for eight hours. He hadn't slept that long in years. He awoke feeling a little odd, but it wasn't an unpleasant feeling. It was something he just hadn't felt in a long, long time. Hope. And overwhelming gratitude for the gift of Mercy.

Ponder

What is distressing you today? What do you long for God to do? Have you experienced similar frustration over ungodliness that the psalmist expresses in this psalm? What do you think the phrase "tremble and do not sin" means? In what ways have you encountered mercy? How does God—and his gifts of mercy and grace—help us sleep and dwell in safety?

PRAY

Answer me when I call to you, my righteous God. Please give me relief from my distress; have mercy on me and hear my prayer. Lord, I feel such shame. I feel such guilt over what I have done. I know that I have failed you so many times. And yet you still want to be near me! Your mercy and grace know no end. You call me to yourself, and you hear me when I call. God of mercy, forgive me for my sin and cleanse my heart. Quiet my mind, my heart, my body. Let me rest in you, for you are my safe place.

—— Paws in His Presence ——

God is full of mercy, and he loves me.

The God Who Knows Us

O LORD, you have examined my heart
and know everything about me.
You know when I sit down or stand up.
You know my thoughts even when I'm far away.
You see me when I travel
and when I rest at home.
You know everything I do.
You know what I am going to say
even before I say it, LORD.
You go before me and follow me.
You place your hand of blessing on my head.
Such knowledge is too wonderful for me,
too great for me to understand!

PSALM 139:1-6

Paws

The door nudged open, revealing a black nose and two deep-brown eyes. A moment later Frankie, a Bernese mountain dog, bounded into the room, his ears bouncing in rhythm with his tongue.

"Hi, buddy," Katrina chuckled. "Sorry I left you, but I had to find a quiet place to get some work done."

The tricolored dog never seemed bothered when he was left alone, but he was always overjoyed to reunite with his human again. Frankie snuggled close and laid his head on Katrina's leg, his dark eyes looking up with such adoration that she felt a lump rise in her throat.

"I don't deserve you, Frankie," she whispered, rubbing her dog's head.

Loyal, dependable, faithful, I'll-always-come-find-you Frankie. The five-year-old gentle giant loved each member of his human family. He loved how Katrina's husband, Daniel, gave him body rubs, finding all the itchy places Frankie couldn't reach to scratch. He loved learning new tricks from fifteen-year-old Zander. And there was no one he loved playing with more than seventeen-year-old Jordan—the family often joked that Frankie looked at Jordan like a littermate. But while the loyal dog loved each and every member of the family, it was Katrina he stuck to like a shadow.

Frankie followed Katrina from room to room.

He waited outside the bathroom door.

He lay at her feet while she worked.

He followed her outside.

He waited in the driveway when Katrina went to the store and would try to jump in her arms when she returned.

And every night, even if he was snuggled in his dog bed downstairs, Frankie would get up and escort Katrina up the stairs when she was ready to go to bed.

Wherever Katrina was, that was where Frankie wanted to be.

Of course, Frankie's tendencies occasionally made for some interesting close calls. Katrina had stubbed her toe more than once trying not to step on her dog. And she'd had several awkward bathroom moments when Frankie would nudge the door open and rush in. But over time, her dog's habit of following her everywhere became one of his most endearing qualities—and a tangible reminder of God's constant presence.

On days when life moved at warp speed, in times of sickness and loneliness, in seasons when it was easy to feel overlooked, forgotten, or unnoticed, Frankie was there.

His eyes looking up.

His tongue hanging out.

His paw resting on Katrina's arm.

To Katrina, his constant presence was a tangible reminder of God's faithfulness and love, and his favorite game of "Find Katrina" was a beautiful picture of God's constant pursuit of his children. Every time she gave Frankie a hug, she thought how wonderful it was to be wrapped in God's perfect love.

Ponder

How does the realization that God knows everything about you make you feel? How might someone's view of God influence how they feel about him seeing and knowing everything they do? What does it mean for God to go before you and to follow you? Spend a few quiet minutes with God. Invite him to examine your heart and make you aware of his loving presence.

PRAY

O Lord, you know my heart. You know me better than anyone. You know me better than I even know myself. You know when I sit down and when I stand up. You know my thoughts, my motivations, my insecurities. You see me when I travel far and when I sit at home. You know everything I do—and you know why I do it. You even know what I'm going to say before the words are formed in my mouth. You go before me and you follow me. You hem me in with your presence. You know me—you really know me— and still you place your loving hand of blessing on me. I can't possibly understand that kind of perfect love, and yet I trust it. I trust you, and I worship you.

Paws in His Presence

God knows everything about me, and he loves me.

The God of Joy

O God, you are my God;
I earnestly search for you.
My soul thirsts for you;
my whole body longs for you
in this parched and weary land
where there is no water.
I have seen you in your sanctuary
and gazed upon your power and glory.
Your unfailing love is better than life itself;
how I praise you!
I will praise you as long as I live,
lifting up my hands to you in prayer.

PSALM 63:1-4

Paws

"Wow! You're not going to believe this. Hunter jumped over his bridge and swam right up to me when he heard your voice through the phone," Lisa's brother, Noah, exclaimed.

Lisa called out a greeting to her nearly six-inch Pictus catfish, thankful that her brother had agreed to hold his phone next to Hunter's aquarium. Noah was surprised—and delighted—at the response of Lisa's aquatic pet. The last time he had watched Hunter when Lisa was on vacation, the fish had barely moved in his tank.

"He's so animated right now," Noah said.

"I guess he wanted to hear my voice," Lisa said proudly.

And indeed, she was proud of the bond she had with the fish her nephew, Mike, had picked out for her several years earlier.

"Pictus catfish are hardy," Mike had said. "Really good for beginners."

Lisa was a novice fish owner at the time, but Mike had enjoyed the hobby for years. She had trusted Mike's advice, which proved to be right. Hunter—named for the Cy Young Award pitcher and Hall of Fame inductee Catfish Hunter—had proven to be very easy to care for and also very intelligent.

"Watch this," Lisa would say to visitors. "Let's get sweeping, Hunter."

At these words, the Pictus catfish would start swimming rapidly around his twenty-gallon tank, stirring up the leftover bits from his previous meal. As he created a whirlpool, Lisa would use a net to collect the food pulled up by the swirling water. Hunter would also play peek-a-boo-I-see-you anytime Lisa came up to his tank.

Lisa loved her fish as much as her cats, and as much as her friends loved their various four-legged pets. But the bond was deeper than just human and animal. The real reason Lisa held such affection for her fish of fifteen years was because he reminded her of her nephew. Soon after Mike had picked out the then-fingerling for his aunt, he passed away unexpectedly. Lisa had been devastated and depressed over Mike's death, and yet the catfish gave her joy, connecting her to the beloved young man she missed.

Several months later, Lisa had an idea. She often sang made-up melodies for the cats. Why not Hunter too? So she started to sing: "Who's my bubbly boy? My Hunter catfish boy?" The fish seemed to love the tune. He swam up to look at her, wiggled his tail, and zoomed around the tank, like a child running around a living room on Christmas morning. He finished his aquatic dance by returning to gaze at Lisa's beaming face on the other side of the glass. The song became part of their daily routine and always brought a smile to Lisa's face.

"You should sing to him!" Lisa now teased her brother on the phone.

"No, thanks. He would much prefer you."

So Lisa sang to her catfish—her pet and friend who helped her rediscover joy and keep the memory of her nephew alive.

Ponder

In what ways did Hunter help Lisa? What is your soul thirsting for and longing for today? How might God's presence meet that longing? What does the psalmist say is better than life itself? What is something you can praise God for today?

O God, you are my God, and I am earnestly seeking you with all my heart. Life feels like a dry and weary land—and my soul is so desperate for a drink from your streams of living water. I am desperate for you, Lord. Through your Word and your world, I have seen a glimpse of you. Still, I long to see you even more. To see you in your sanctuary and gaze upon your power and glory. Father, your unfailing love is better than life itself. Because of your love I will praise you as long as I live. I will lift up my hands to you in prayer and thanksgiving, for your love is better than life.

Paws in His Presence

God's love brings joy to my soul.

The God Who Gives Courage

Lord, I have many enemies!
Many people have turned against me.
Many people are talking about me.
They say, "God won't rescue him."
But, Lord, you are my shield.
You are my wonderful God who gives me courage.
I will pray to the Lord.
And he will answer me from his holy mountain.
I can lie down and go to sleep.
And I will wake up again
because the Lord protects me.
Thousands of enemies may surround me.
But I am not afraid.

PSALM 3:1-6, ICB

Paws

"It's okay, Kip," Alisha tried to assure the family's Jack Russell terrier cowering behind a chair. "Hayden's okay. He just has some extra stuff with him."

Alisha's throat burned as her eyes scanned the room—medicine, bandages, and post–liver transplant pamphlets covered the coffee table. A metal walker was pushed against the back wall, and a tall, shiny IV pole towered over her six-year-old son, Hayden, as he slept on the sofa.

Alisha had never felt more weary. Her entire body ached. She hadn't slept in a real bed in weeks, but now that they were back home, terror gripped her heart, making sleep impossible. *Will I really be able to give Hayden the care he needs?* She had closely watched the nurses clean and care for Hayden's incisions as well as the port used to administer the multiple medications and large amount of fluids his body needed.

She had done the routine in front of the nurses several times, but now that the medical staff were gone, she worried she wouldn't be enough for her son. Her precious, brave boy who had battled a genetic liver disease throughout his young life. Gratitude and grief filled her heart as she thought of the family who had made the lifesaving decision to donate their child's liver to her son. It was a sacrifice and gift she would never take for granted. *God, hold them close and strengthen them,* she prayed from her heart.

A yelp from behind Alisha's favorite chair brought her attention back to the present situation. Hayden had been in the hospital for three weeks and now that he was finally home, he couldn't wait to see his canine buddy, Kip. It was all Hayden had talked about for the last few days. Alisha had wanted the reunion to go smoothly for her son who had endured so much. But the normally happy-go-lucky terrier who followed Hayden everywhere had been spooked by the IV pole and disappeared behind the chair. Kip was too scared to come out and say hello. Alisha was thankful that Hayden was too exhausted to notice and had fallen asleep on the sofa a few minutes after his arrival.

"Come here, boy," Alisha's husband, Terrance, quietly called Kip.

Kip took two steps, then darted back behind the chair.

"Come, Kip," Alisha tried.

Kip bounced on his front legs—clearly wanting to obey, but his fear kept him rooted in place.

Wanting desperately to do something for her son—and not wanting him to wake up to find his dog afraid to be near him—Alisha sat on the floor next to Hayden. She watched him sleep for a few minutes. His face, though swollen from the medications, was still the most precious face she had ever seen.

Alisha patted the floor beside her. "Kip-Kip, do you want to come say hi to Hayden?" she asked softly.

Kip peeked around the side of the chair. He sniffed the air. He looked at Alisha. He looked at Terrance. His gaze landed on his boy—Hayden.

Kip took a few tentative steps. Then a few more. He eyed the IV pole and gave it a wide berth as he crouched his way to Alisha. He sniffed the metal base of the towering intruder. He smelled Alisha's jeans. He climbed onto her lap to get a better view of Hayden.

"He missed you, Kip," Terrance said, on the sofa at Hayden's feet.

"He needs his best bud," Alisha added.

Kip put his front legs on the sofa and leaned in to smell Hayden. He sniffed his arm, he watched his chest, he licked his hand.

Hayden's eyes fluttered open. "Kip?"

The brown-and-white dog licked his hand again. He climbed onto the sofa and snuggled next to his boy. Hayden smiled. It was the first smile Alisha had seen on his face in weeks. Hayden rested his arm against his dog, mumbled, "I'm home, Kip," and fell back asleep.

Alisha kissed Kip's head. "Good boy, Kip," she said, leaning her own head against the sofa.

A few minutes later Alisha was sound asleep too—right beside her boy and his dog.

Ponder

When was the last time you felt fearful of something? What gave you courage during that time? In what ways does God act as our shield? How might God give us courage? How was the psalmist able to have courage in the midst of terrifying circumstances?

PRAY

Lord, I feel like I am surrounded by enemies. Enemies of my peace, my joy, my comfort, my integrity, and my reputation. It feels like I have no one in my corner, no one I can trust. No one to encourage me or help me. But . . . I have you! And you are more than enough. You are my shield. You protect my heart; you give life to my soul. You are my wonderful God who fills my weary heart with courage. I know I can pray to you, and you will hear me. I trust you to answer in the way that is best. I can rest in you. I can face another day because you are with me. No matter what happens, you are my God, and you love me. Those truths give me courage to face another day.

Paws in His Presence

When I am afraid,
I can trust God to help me and give me courage.

The God Who
Provides Contentment

LORD, my heart is not proud;
my eyes are not haughty.
I don't concern myself with matters too great
or too awesome for me to grasp.
Instead, I have calmed and quieted myself,
like a weaned child who no longer cries for its mother's milk.
Yes, like a weaned child is my soul within me.
O Israel, put your hope in the LORD—
now and always.

PSALM 131:1-3

Paws

Twelve newborn puppies wriggled and squeaked as they nursed.

"Good job, Wrigley," Marie cheered her exhausted Golden retriever. "You did a very good job."

Wrigley let out a forceful sigh and laid her head on Marie's knee.

"Mama, I love this one!" Her five-year-old son, Luke, exclaimed, pointing to the male puppy with the red ribbon. "And that one," he added, pointing to the female with the purple ribbon. "And that one, and that one . . . I love all of them!"

Marie, suddenly feeling as tired as Wrigley, smiled at her son.

"Me too, buddy."

Marie leaned her head against the plywood birthing box they had created for Wrigley and her puppies and closed her eyes, overcome by weariness.

The past few months had been some of the most trying of her life. She still felt nauseated when she thought about the horrific car accident her husband and son had been in, both of them taken to the hospital. Never in her life had she been so scared. That was until just a few weeks later, when Luke became so ill that he had to be hospitalized again. It had taken several agonizing days for the doctors to identify the virus that had made her little boy so sick.

A shiver of fear—and what she imagined a therapist would call post-traumatic stress—rippled through her body. Her hands tingled. Her chest tightened. *God, why?* her heart cried for the hundredth time. *Why did all of that happen to my little boy? Why didn't you intervene?*

The puppy wearing an orange ribbon fell from the nursing pile in a milk-induced slumber. He flopped beside Marie's foot—his tiny little tongue sticking out, the fuzz around his mouth tinged with milk. The little guy was the definition of full and satisfied.

"Can I pet him?" Luke asked, his pleading eyes filled with hopeful expectation.

Oh, how she loved those eyes. Her own filled with gratitude. She might never understand the why behind the accident or illness, but in that moment, she realized she didn't need to. Instead, she would focus on the gift she had been given—the pain she had been spared—and she would relish the moments that she had with her son, her husband, and the menagerie of animals they lived with, including the adorable little puppies currently in various states of milk comas.

"Of course you can pet him, buddy," she assured Luke. "I know you will be super gentle with these little ones. You're like a big brother to them."

Luke beamed at his mom, then turned his attention to the puppy wearing the orange ribbon. He ran his finger lightly down its soft back, then let out an adorable giggle as a green-ribboned puppy stuck his head in the pocket of Luke's shorts.

"This is the best day ever!" Luke declared.

Marie could not agree more.

Ponder

What "great matters" concern your soul today? Have you ever longed to know why God allowed something or didn't prevent something from happening in your life? What does this psalm teach us about finding contentment in the not-knowing? How does a humble trust in God calm and quiet your soul? What does it mean to put your hope in God?

Lord, help me pursue humility and grace. Keep pride and arrogance far from me. Help me to accept your will and to pursue your ways. Calm and quieten my heart with your love. Steady my soul with your presence. You are my hope and my safe place, both now and forevermore. I trust you, Lord. Amen.

Paws in His Presence

God can calm and quieten my soul.

The God Who
Supplies Generously

Good comes to those who lend money generously
and conduct their business fairly.
Such people will not be overcome by evil.
Those who are righteous will be long remembered.
They do not fear bad news;
they confidently trust the LORD to care for them.
They are confident and fearless
and can face their foes triumphantly.
They share freely and give generously to those in need.
Their good deeds will be remembered forever.
They will have influence and honor.

PSALM 112:5-9

Paws

Camille didn't set out to attract woodland creatures to her backyard. She didn't intend to fill one wall of her garage with birdseed, nectar, cracked corn, and suet cakes. But once she had, she couldn't imagine life any other way.

It all started with one bird feeder, bought online during the pandemic.

"It's getting a bit lonely around here," Camille had said to her cat, Brontë, while scrolling online through bird feeder options. "We have these nice big glass doors and that big open yard. How about we set out some birdseed so we can watch them eat?"

Meow.

Camille appreciated her cat's agreeableness.

She placed the order for a feeder and birdseed and eagerly awaited their arrival. Two days later she hung the feeder from a tree branch easily seen through the sliding glass doors. She filled it with wild birdseed mix and dashed back inside to watch the flock of birds arrive.

It turned out to be more of a trickle than a flock at first, but over the next two days word spread throughout the wild kingdom, and her feeder was soon in high demand. Brontë enjoyed lying in sun puddles inside the house, watching the frenzy of activity taking place just outside her doors. And Camille found unexpected joy in tending the feeder each day.

Soon, two more feeders and a birdbath were added to the lineup, more birdseed was ordered, and Brontë and Camille began spending time outside with the birds. Camille would feed Brontë, then open the sliding glass doors to let her putter around the backyard while Camille refilled the feeders. She loved watching Brontë watch the birds. The cat never tried to chase them. Never made any move against them. She was simply content to watch their comings and goings.

One day, as Camille and Brontë were dawdling outside, a rabbit hopped into the backyard.

"Brontë . . . ," Camille said, turning to check on her cat—who was lying on the deck without a care in the world.

The rabbit hopped under the bird feeder and started investigating the dropped seed. That gave Camille an idea. The next day, she set out some lettuce and carrots under the feeder. That evening, the rabbit was back. Camille and Brontë sat on the deck and watched the newcomer eat his fill below the feeding birds.

The next week, two ducks waddled into Camille's yard. The male duck startled Brontë, who gave a half-hearted chase before plopping down on the grass. The next day the ducks were back, and Camille was prepared. She had purchased cracked corn, and after reading that ducks like grapes, she sprinkled cut grapes on top of the corn that she had scattered under the bird feeder.

She and Brontë relaxed on the deck and watched a parade of animals, including a squirrel and two chipmunks, partake of the delectable buffet.

Camille loved watching the animals eat—she loved being able to provide a safe respite for them. But what she loved most of all was how they treated each other. They didn't fight, squabble, or chase. They didn't squawk, hiss, or grunt. They simply ate—together.

Trusting there would be enough. Trusting their needs would be met.

Soon, the rabbits began sleeping in Camille's yard, while Brontë lounged on the deck. Their presence, along with all of the creatures, became a beautiful reminder to Camille of the peace that can be found through trust and generosity. Trust in God to provide and generosity to share his provision with others.

It was a lesson she didn't expect to learn during a pandemic that brought headlines of fear and stories of hoarding. But it was a lesson she was most grateful for. And one she and Brontë continue to be reminded of daily as their backyard regulars enjoy a meal and rest peacefully nearby.

Ponder

In what ways have you experienced generosity? How have you been generous recently? Do you agree that generosity grows as your trust in God grows? Why do you think that is the case? What is a need that you can surrender to God today? Will you trust him to provide for you?

PRAY

Father, open my hands to those in need, and guard my heart against selfish gain and greed. Keep my eyes and my heart fixed on you and let me be known as a person of integrity who has earnest faith in you. Help me to trust you more than I fear anything, even all of the imagined worst-case scenarios my mind conjures up. Let me live and act out of the abundance of grace you have provided for me. Make me confident and fearless in you. And Lord, as my trust in you grows, may my generosity grow as well. Help me share your love and your goodness with those around me.

Paws in His Presence

God's generosity toward me enables me
to be generous to others.

The God Who Redeems

*I wait for the L*ORD*, my whole being waits,*
and in his word I put my hope.
*I wait for the L*ORD
more than watchmen wait for the morning,
more than watchmen wait for the morning.
*Israel, put your hope in the L*ORD*,*
*for with the L*ORD *is unfailing love*
and with him is full redemption.
He himself will redeem Israel
from all their sins.

PSALM 130:5-8, NIV

Paws

"We'll be home soon, girl," Bridget told her five-year-old beagle, Samoa.

"We love you, Samoa!" Bridget's six-year-old daughter, Delaney, called out, skipping toward the garage.

The brown-and-white beagle stood in the kitchen tilting her head to the left, to the right, then back to the left. When Bridget took her keys from the hook by the door, Samoa's body stilled. Her dark eyes lowered in resignation.

"I promise we will be back before you know it," Bridget said, giving her dog's head one more pat.

Samoa remained motionless as Bridget and Delaney walked into the garage. However, Bridget knew the moment she closed the door, Samoa would run to the front window to watch them leave.

Sure enough, a moment later, as Bridget backed out of the driveway, their dog appeared in the front window.

"She looks so sad," Delaney observed. "I wish we could bring her to my recital."

"I know," Bridget agreed. "But I don't think your piano teacher would appreciate us bringing a dog into the music center."

Yet, knowing how much Samoa missed her human family when they were gone, a part of Bridget wished she *could* take the dog with them. Since joining their family as a young puppy, Samoa had established a place in her pack that consisted of Delaney, Bridget, and her husband, Rick. Samoa had always been happiest and most content when they were all together, and she could be vocal and destructive whenever they weren't.

It had taken a long time for Samoa to learn to trust that when her human pack had to leave without her, they would always return home.

Younger Samoa would whine and cry and chew things up in distress when she was alone. When the separation was for a longer period of time, they would crate her to minimize damage to the house. The smaller contained space seemed to comfort her somewhat. But Bridget and Rick continued to work hard to build Samoa's separation tolerance so she could enjoy greater freedom and have more room to move around.

They tried many things—a compression vest, calming chews, positive reinforcement, and keeping the television tuned to the Animal Planet channel whenever they left. But what seemed to help the most was the simple repetition of always coming back. As she grew older, Samoa learned to trust and count on her family's promise. Bridget liked to think that their smart beagle had discovered that her temporary sadness would eventually be replaced with a joyous homecoming.

And that was exactly what happened when Bridget and Delaney returned home from the piano recital. Bridget gave two quick beeps of the horn when she pulled into the driveway.

"There she is!" Delaney cheered as their dog appeared in the window. A few minutes later, Bridget and Delaney walked into the kitchen and Samoa came bounding toward them—a toy in her mouth and a happy wag to her tail.

"Come on, Samoa!" Delaney shouted, running to their upright piano. "I'll play my recital song for you."

With Samoa's joy fully restored, she eagerly followed Delaney into the family room to receive her private performance—which she enjoyed from the bench, right beside her girl.

Ponder

What are you waiting on God to do? What does it mean to put our hope in God's Word? Read John 1:1 and 1:14. How do these verses relate to the first two lines of today's portion from Psalm 130? How might a watchman feel as he waited for morning to come? Have you ever anxiously awaited the dawning of a new day? Or longed for an end to a season of darkness? How would you define "full redemption"? What do you long for God to redeem?

PRAY

I wait for you, Lord. My whole being waits for you. My hope is in your Word and the true hope of your Son, Jesus. I wait expectantly for you, like a night watchman awaits the morning. I long for you to scatter the darkness with your redeeming light. Hold me in your unfailing love. Keep my hope secure in you. Forgive my sin and redeem all that has been lost and broken. I need you, God, and I trust you. In Jesus' name, amen.

Paws in His Presence

I can put my hope in God;
he will redeem all that is lost and broken.

The God Who Shepherds Us

The LORD is my shepherd;
I have all that I need.
He lets me rest in green meadows;
he leads me beside peaceful streams.
He renews my strength.
He guides me along right paths,
bringing honor to his name.
Even when I walk
through the darkest valley,
I will not be afraid,
for you are close beside me.
Your rod and your staff
protect and comfort me.
You prepare a feast for me
in the presence of my enemies.
You honor me by anointing my head with oil.
My cup overflows with blessings.
Surely your goodness and unfailing love will pursue me
all the days of my life,
and I will live in the house of the LORD
forever.

PSALM 23

Paws

"I can't remember the last time I laughed this hard," Jenaye said, clutching her middle.

She leaned forward and a baby goat leaped onto her back causing Jenaye to jump—and the three friends who had gone with her to the goat farm to howl with laughter.

The visit to the farm had been a last-minute idea, but one Jenaye knew would live on forever—both in their memories and in the countless photos they had taken.

The past year had been difficult for each of them. Each woman had walked through painful seasons—grief, job stress, relationship issues, and anxiety. So when an opportunity arose for them to spend the day together, they knew they wanted to make it special.

They thought about visiting a museum or maybe the zoo. They tossed around potential itineraries involving parks, shopping, and new restaurants. But when a coworker mentioned a farm that allowed people to cuddle with goats, the group of friends knew they had found their destination.

The owner of the farm welcomed them warmly and gave them a brief tour and overview of goat cuddling etiquette. She passed out yoga mats to sit on, then led them to a small, fenced area where she deposited seven baby goats among them. The goats ranged in age from three weeks to three months and varied in temperament from sleepy-headed cuddle-bugs to hyperactive four-legged gymnasts.

Jenaye selected a tiny cinnamon-colored goat named Bess. The three-week-old goat dozed in her arms while the more energetic goat kids pranced around the yard, climbed in her friends' laps, and chewed fallen leaves.

"This is just what we needed," Selina said, laughing as a black goat named Zorro tried to jump on her back.

"Goat cuddles make everything better," Eliza interjected—a moment before a grayish-white goat named Casper began chomping on her hair.

"Um . . . guys! A little help . . . ," Cameron squeaked.

The group turned in her direction and burst out laughing to find not one, but two goats standing on her back. Jenaye laid Bess on the grass and rushed to off-load the animals from Cameron. But each time Jenaye removed a goat, it jumped back on.

"Stay," she tried to command with a serious tone before hilarity took over.

Seeing the fun jungle gym their siblings had discovered, more baby goats ran to Cameron. She and her friends cried tears of laughter as they tried in vain to free Cameron from the impromptu goat mosh pit. Eventually, the goats were enticed by Eliza holding a particularly delicious looking clump of leaves, and they followed her and the foliage away from Cameron.

The foursome wiped dirt, grass, and parting gifts from the goats from their clothes, arms, and hands, then sat back on their yoga mats to catch their breath.

"I couldn't have made it through this year without all of you," Jenaye said. Gratitude filled her heart for the friends God had brought into her life five years earlier. Friends she had come to love dearly and depend on in ways she hadn't known she needed. "God gave me such a gift when he gave me you."

"Group hug!" As they leaned in, three goats leaped onto their shoulders.

"God, good friends, and goats," Selina chuckled. "What else does a person need?"

They spent the next hour laughing, joking, and thanking God for his faithful presence, as well as his gifts of friendship—and baby goats.

Ponder

Are you in a quiet season of green meadows and peaceful streams? Or are you walking through a dark valley? How has God been shepherding you through this current season of life? What gifts and blessings has he given that have helped you through the dark valleys? What are some green meadow and peaceful stream moments you've experienced recently? Take a moment to reflect on God's goodness and faithful presence.

PRAY

Lord, you are the Good Shepherd who leads and guides me and who provides all that I truly need. Thank you for the gift of your presence—the sacred place where my heart can find true rest. Please renew my strength today. Hold fast to my hand and help me live for you. And even when darkness comes—when it becomes hard to see your face—help me remember who you are and that you are right beside me. Lord, help me also trust that you are always at work in the world and in my life. Remind me that you are working all things together for my good and your glory. Keep my heart and mind focused on you, help me be grateful for all the wonderful gifts you have given, and remind me that because I trust in you, I will be with you forever.

--- Paws in His Presence ---

God is the Good Shepherd who leads me
and guides me through life.

The God Who Guides

Let the morning bring me word of your unfailing love,
for I have put my trust in you.
Show me the way I should go,
for to you I entrust my life.
Rescue me from my enemies, LORD,
for I hide myself in you.
Teach me to do your will,
for you are my God;
may your good Spirit
lead me on level ground.
For your name's sake, LORD, preserve my life;
in your righteousness, bring me out of trouble.
In your unfailing love, silence my enemies;
destroy all my foes,
for I am your servant.

PSALM 143:8-12, NIV

Paws

Rosie raced down the stairs with an enthusiasm Kara did not share. The sun had barely risen, and Kara was still wiping sleep from her eyes, yet her five-year-old labradoodle's eyes were wide with excitement, her ears perked with possibilities of adventure.

Rosie ran to her bowl—preferring to eat before doing anything else. Her tail swung with anticipation of the crunchy kibble from the cup in Kara's hand. As Rosie inhaled her breakfast, Kara inhaled the aroma coming from her coffee maker. After pouring herself a generous cup and handing Rosie her after-breakfast dental treat, Kara opened the back door and followed her dog outside.

The cool morning air in late spring held the promise of summer. Birds flitted and fluttered at the feeder. Leaves swayed in a slight breeze.

But Rosie paid them no attention—at least not yet. First, she had someone special to greet.

Meow!

India, the family's outdoor cat, rose from her favorite cushion, stretched her front legs, and walked over to meet Rosie in the middle of the deck. Rosie lowered her head to bump noses with India, then stood perfectly still as the cat weaved in and out of her legs, rubbing her gray-and-black face against Rosie's sand-colored fur. Their routine had become such a familiar part of their morning that on the rare occasions India wasn't on the deck, Kara and Rosie would stare at each other, unsure what they were supposed to do next.

After India finished her rubs, Rosie sniffed her from nose to tail—a canine investigation into India's late-night activities. The two spent several minutes together, inspecting each other, rubbing against each other, and peering out into the vast expanse of the backyard together.

As they did, Kara lifted her face toward the rising sun and whispered, "Good morning, God."

Kara had a busy day ahead and felt the pressure of the clock, but her heart craved this time with God as much as her animals craved greeting each other. Their routine had become as necessary as it was familiar. Her animal friends' excitement to start their day with each other had become her own daily reminder to begin her days acknowledging and praying to the one who knew her and loved her more than any other—and whose Spirit she depended on to guide her throughout the day.

Ponder

Is spending focused time with God part of your morning routine? If not, would you be willing to spend a few minutes each morning this week acknowledging and thinking about him? How has God revealed his unfailing love to you in the past? In what ways does God show us the way we should go? How might focusing your heart and mind on God in the morning equip you to face enemies—both internal and external—throughout your day?

Lord, I look to you this morning. Please remind me of your unfailing love and help me put my trust in you. Please show me the way I should go. God, I trust you with my life and ask that you would rescue me from anyone or anything that seeks to hurt me— even if those are my own negative thoughts. Hide me in your presence and teach me to do your will. Lead me in your way—the way of truth and love. Lord, take control of my life and be glorified in me.

Paws in His Presence

God loves me; I can trust him to guide me through my days.

The God Whose
Love Never Ends

Give thanks to the LORD, for he is good.
His love endures forever.
Give thanks to the God of gods.
His love endures forever.
Give thanks to the Lord of lords:
His love endures forever.
to him who alone does great wonders.
His love endures forever.

PSALM 136:1-4, NIV

Paws

Samantha was so in love with her hound-mix, Gunner, that a part of her thought her beloved dog would live forever. But when fourteen-year-old Gunner's health rapidly declined, reality crashed in on her and she began pleading with God to spare him.

"God, I need him. Please don't take him from me."

Even as she begged God to heal her dog, her mind begrudgingly began to accept what her heart still couldn't: Her precious companion was in horrible pain and needed her to let him go.

"I can't live without you," she sobbed while he lay on his bed, unable to get up. "How am I going to make it without you?"

His tired eyes looked up at her, and she knew. She knew Gunner needed her to do what was best *for him*. To put *him* first, as he had always put her first. She buried her head against his side and cried.

"I will always, always love you. You are the bestest boy in the whole entire world, and I will never forget you."

The vet came to the house the next day, and Samantha did what she never thought she could—she let Gunner go.

She thought her heart would break under the crushing weight of his absence. It felt as if the very ground beneath her feet had shifted. Her entire life had revolved around Gunner—especially in the later years as his care required more of her time.

She went through her days aimlessly. She couldn't bear the thought of moving any of Gunner's things. She carefully collected his hair from the floor, wanting to save every strand. And she spent hours scrolling through pictures of him on her phone.

Her friends reached out with condolences and sent sympathy cards. She appreciated their thoughtfulness, and yet, all she really wanted was to have Gunner back.

A few weeks after losing her beloved companion, she received a card from a local animal rescue organization informing her that a donation had been made in Gunner's name to help with the care of a dog with special needs. Overwhelmed by the gesture, Samantha clutched the card to her heart. She called her friends to thank them.

"Gunner might be gone, but his legacy isn't," her friend Caroline said. "His legacy lives on in you, and now he's also giving a young dog a chance at a good life."

Samantha's heart pounded with gratitude and resolution. Her grief was too raw to allow her to go back to the animal shelter where she had volunteered for years, but she would go back someday—for Gunner.

She would donate to dog rescue organizations—for Gunner.

She would allow herself to grieve and to live—for Gunner.

She would forgive God for not allowing her dog to live forever—for Gunner.

She would choose to be grateful for the time she had with him—for Gunner.

And a year-and-a half after losing the best boy in the whole wide world, she cautiously opened her heart up to a young Lab-mix in need of a home—for Gunner.

The skittish black dog had been found starving and dehydrated. She needed a home, and the shelter where Samantha used to volunteer reached out to her.

Samantha hesitated. She wanted Gunner back, not a new dog. She had given her whole heart to him. Would there be anything left for another dog?

It wasn't an instant connection. She had built protective walls around her wounded heart. But she was willing to try, willing to open her heart again—for Gunner.

"You would have loved your big brother," Samantha told the dog she named Scout, several weeks after bringing her home. Scout offered Samantha her belly.

Samantha smiled, remembering all the belly rubs she had given Gunner over the years. She knew it was going to take a while for her to fully love Scout, but she knew she would—for Gunner.

Ponder

Have you experienced the loss of a beloved pet? In what ways do you continue to honor the bond you shared with them? Why is it important to continue to give thanks to God even when facing difficult circumstances? In what ways might remembering God's enduring love help fill our hearts with gratitude? What can you thank God for today?

PRAY

God, you are so good. I praise you for who you are. Even in hard circumstances, I praise you. And I thank you that your love endures forever. Sovereign Lord, you are holy and righteous. You are over all and above all. Help me remember that nothing is impossible for you. And when the days get hard, help my heart and mind to find comfort in knowing that your perfect love endures forever.

Paws in His Presence

God's perfect love endures forever.

The God Who Saves

Troubles have come again and again.
They sound like waterfalls.
Your waves are crashing
all around me.
The Lord shows his true love every day.
At night I have a song,
and I pray to my living God.
I say to God, my Rock,
"Why have you forgotten me?
Why am I sad
and troubled by my enemies?"
My enemies' insults make me feel
as if my bones were broken.
They are always saying,
"Where is your God?"
Why am I so sad?
Why am I so upset?
I should put my hope in God.
I should keep praising him,
my Savior and my God.

PSALM 42:7-11, ICB

Paws

"You're a natural in the water," Kaitlin said, beaming at her dog, Bubba, swimming in the choppy waves where the Atlantic meets the Gulf of Mexico.

It was the first time she had taken her recently adopted pit bull/terrier-mix to the beach, and she hadn't been sure how the dog would respond to the water. In fact, she had been quite nervous that he wouldn't enjoy the experience since the approximately three-year-old dog had been rescued from a shelter that had been flooded during Hurricane Irma. But instead of showing a fear response, her black dog with the white patch on his chest had darted into the crashing waves with such exuberance that Kaitlin suspected it was something he had done many times before.

"I'm so glad you like it," Kaitlin chuckled as Bubba swam back to shore only to turn around and head right back into the water. Kaitlin had always loved the water. So much so that she was currently working as a medical assistant at the Dolphin Research Center. Since the ocean was such a huge part of her life, she was thrilled she would be able to share it with her new dog.

Bubba swam out to retrieve every tennis ball she threw; he ran in the surf and dug in the sand. But Kaitlin was completely unprepared for what her dog did when she decided to swim into deeper water. Kaitlin was a strong swimmer and enjoyed being out far enough to practice her freestyle stroke. Bubba, however, saw the situation differently. He seemed to interpret his human's rotating arms and kicking legs as a signal for help. Bubba's leash was attached to his swimming vest in case she needed to grab him, but now he had the end of his leash in his mouth, heading toward her. Once there, he dropped it near her hand.

Kaitlin could hardly believe what she was seeing.

"Are you trying to save me?"

Curious as to what her dog would do, she held the end of the leash in her hand and waited. A moment later, Bubba was swimming with purpose to the shore, pulling her behind him.

"You saved me!" Kaitlin exclaimed, throwing her arms around him. "Just to be clear, I wasn't actually drowning," she chuckled, "but you saved me! You are Bubba the Superhero!"

Thinking his behavior was an amusing coincidence, she didn't think much about it again until the following weekend when some friends decided to meet up at the beach with their dogs. Bubba leapt from the car and pulled Kaitlin all the way to the sand. She let his leash drag behind him as he ran into the surf. He frolicked with the other dogs for a while, but then swam out just beyond the waves to where Kaitlin's friend, Lauren, was swimming. He dropped the end of his leash by her hand, and when she grabbed it, Bubba began swimming her back to shore.

"I think he just rescued me!" Lauren said.

For the next half hour as Kaitlin swam with her friends, Bubba made half a dozen "rescues," even circling back when someone dropped the leash to replace it in their hand.

"Bubba the lifeguard! He'll save you whether you need it or not," her friend, Joe, said with a laugh.

They laughed even harder when the self-appointed canine lifeguard attempted to rescue a stranger doing laps. The older man was quite startled when Bubba interrupted his swim. Kaitlin called out, "Sorry! My dog thinks you're in trouble and need a tow back to shore."

She called Bubba to swim back, but he hesitated. He looked at the man, then at Kaitlin, then back at the man. A moment later, Bubba proudly towed the stranger back to shore.

"Well, I was getting a bit tired, so thank you, pup," the man said, patting Bubba's head.

Kaitlin reached into her bag and tossed her canine lifeguard a treat.

"And here I was thinking I was the rescuer for bringing you out of that shelter. But clearly you are the real hero here."

She rubbed his chest, grateful to know if she ever did find herself struggling in the waves, Bubba would be there to get her safely to shore.

Ponder

Have you ever needed rescue? How did God provide for you in that season? What emotions are evoked in you when you read the first two lines of this psalm? What troubles are you facing today? Have you ever felt forgotten by God? What did the psalmist instruct his heart to do when he felt forgotten by God? How might you instruct your soul to put your hope in God today? What evidence of God's love can you see?

PRAY

Lord, it seems like troubles come one right after another. They hit me with the intensity of an unexpected riptide. It feels like I'm being tossed by choppy waves and pulled by crosscurrents. And yet, I know you are with me. I know you love me—you show me your love every day. Even so, Lord, it is so easy for me to forget your love when my circumstances toss me to and fro. At times it feels like you've forgotten me altogether. God, interrupt my negative thoughts. Set me straight so that I might remember who you are and all that you have done. Instruct my heart to put my hope in you. Grant me strength to keep trusting you and praising you, my Savior and my God.

Paws in His Presence

God is my Savior; I can trust him.

The God Who Never Changes

The LORD is a great God,
a great King above all gods.
He holds in his hands the depths of the earth
and the mightiest mountains.
The sea belongs to him, for he made it.
His hands formed the dry land, too.
Come, let us worship and bow down.
Let us kneel before the LORD our maker,
for he is our God.
We are the people he watches over,
the flock under his care.

PSALM 95:3-7

Paws

Happy tears filled Jen's eyes as the plane touched down on the small Caribbean island where she had spent two weeks every summer of her childhood, visiting family and getting to know the place where her mother was born. She hadn't been back on the island in close to twenty years—and she had worried that it wouldn't feel the same. But as she stepped from the small plane and inhaled the sweet-smelling air, her worries disappeared.

"Hi," she whispered to the island she loved.

After dropping off their bags at the condo, Jen led her family down the beach toward the property her aunt and uncle had owned until her uncle's death several years earlier. A fresh pang of grief washed over Jen as she thought about losing her aunt less than a year ago. Oh, how she missed them.

She gathered herself during the short walk to her aunt and uncle's former house.

"The beach in front of their house is one of my favorite places on earth," Jen said, suddenly feeling like a teenager again. "I would lie in a hammock under the sea grape trees for hours. Sometimes Iggy—the iguana who lived there—would come down and visit me. I'd always take bread for him." She smiled at the memory. "It was always nice and breezy out there. I can't wait for you to . . ."

Jen stopped. Her mouth dropped. Her breath caught. Her happy place was unrecognizable.

The pristine beach of her childhood was completely overgrown. Gone were the sea grape trees. Gone was the sugar-soft sand. Gone was the dock where she would lie and watch for shooting stars while talking to God and feeling his presence in a way she experienced only there. She peered through the foliage and underbrush for a glimpse of the house where she had made so many happy memories.

"It's gone," she whimpered. "It's all . . . gone."

"Sorry, Mom," her son said.

"The water is still really pretty," her daughter offered.

Her husband put his arm around her and gave her shoulders a squeeze.

Jen's throat tightened. Her hands began to tingle. An emotional dam threatened to break. She had been holding so much in these past few years—grief, anxieties, hurts, fears. But now, staring at the place she had visited in her mind so many times as she tried to cope with the realities of life, she felt her walls begin to crumble, and emotions began to trickle out.

So much had changed over the past twenty years. Loved ones were gone; her parents were aging; her kids would soon head to college; friends had moved away; church even felt different recently. Jen took a steadying breath and led her family back up the beach.

As they sat poolside at the condo applying sunscreen, a large grayish-green iguana emerged from a nearby bush.

"Mom! Is that Iggy?" Jen's daughter exclaimed.

Jen laughed and started to shake her head, but a memory of her uncle hand-feeding Iggy floated through her mind.

"Iguanas can live up to ninety years," he had said in his rhythmic accent of the Caymans. "So this guy could outlive me."

Jen studied the black-footed iguana who studied her in return. His bumpy head tilted to the side. His claws sunk into the sand. He was one of the largest iguanas Jen had ever seen.

"Could you be . . . Iggy?" Jen whispered.

The iguana watched her for another minute, then crossed the pool deck and settled in the shade of a sea grape tree. Jen wiped a tear away and chuckled. *Leave it to me to get emotional about a reptile.*

A moment later, she was drenched from her kids cannonballing into the pool. They might be in their late teens, but they would always be her goofball babies.

Jen dried her sunglasses and looked at the breathtaking view she had loved since childhood. She inhaled deeply.

Yes, the beach from her childhood was different, life was different—*she* was different. But as she looked out over the same turquoise waters she had fallen in love with as a child, she realized that the God who made the waters was still the same God she had talked to from the dock. Thanks to an iguana—and the kind God who sent it—Jen felt wrapped in divine peace and comforted by God's faithfulness. And later that afternoon, she also felt compelled to take some bread down to the reptile who had touched her heart.

Ponder

Do you have a happy place you retreat to in your mind? Where is that? What feelings does that place evoke? When have you felt closest to God? What has changed in your life since then? What has stayed the same? How has God shown his faithfulness to you? In what ways does God's faithfulness comfort and reassure you?

PRAY

Lord, you are great and above all others. You hold the earth and all that is in it in your hands. From the highest mountains to the deepest oceans, you have made it all and you sustain it all. You alone are worthy of our worship and praise. I kneel before you; I bow in worship and adoration. For you are my God, and I am your child. I trust you to care and provide for me.

Paws in His Presence

God is great, and he never changes.

The God Who Delights Our Soul

Blessed is the one
who does not walk in step with the wicked
or stand in the way that sinners take
or sit in the company of mockers,
but whose delight is in the law of the LORD,
and who meditates on his law day and night.
That person is like a tree planted by streams of water,
which yields its fruit in season
and whose leaf does not wither—
whatever they do prospers.

PSALM 1:1-3, NIV

Paws

The cream-colored English Labrador retriever named Gracie slept soundly at Larry's feet, just as she had every morning for nearly fifteen years. These quiet times with his dog had become a sacred part of his day. Gracie's faithful presence during his early morning prayer time served as a living, breathing reminder of God's perfect faithfulness and love.

Gracie rolled to her side and laid her head on Larry's foot. He reached down and stroked his Lab's velvety soft ears. Even as he relished the time with his canine companion, a pang of anticipatory grief squeezed his heart. How much longer would Gracie be a part of his morning time with God? At almost fifteen years of age, Larry knew he had already had more time with his dog than most, but no amount of time would be enough. After all, Gracie wasn't just a pet—she was a therapy dog who had brought hope, comfort, and love to thousands of people.

Photos of Gracie in her red therapy-dog vest—surrounded by a beautiful array of smiling faces—dotted his desk. The gentle-natured dog had logged thousands of hours of therapy visits and impacted many lives—Larry's most of all. And while the senior Lab hadn't been on an official visit in well over a year, Larry knew her legacy would continue to impact people for many years to come.

Larry picked up a photo of puppy Gracie looking up in anticipation at the camera. She had been so easy to train, so eager to learn, so driven to please. Her eyes—her soulful, chocolate brown eyes—had always been focused on him. Always awaiting his instruction. Always ready to offer comfort and reveal a glimmer of hope to a hurting soul.

Larry lowered himself to the floor to sit beside his dog—his Grace.

"I love you, Gracie," he said, allowing his tears to fall—her thick coat catching each one, absorbing his emotion just like she had for a decade and a half. "I don't know how much longer I'll get to have you in my lap, but you will always—always—be in my heart. My beautiful, amazing Grace."

Ponder

What delights you? What do you find yourself thinking about as you wake up and as you fall asleep? What does it mean to delight in the law of the Lord? In what ways might delighting in God and meditating on him bring blessing? How will Gracie's legacy live on, even after she's gone? What do you hope your legacy will be? What can you do today in support of leaving a godly legacy?

PRAY

Almighty God, you are the true source of joy and delight. Let me find my delight in you—in worshipping you, in thinking about you, in obeying you. Open my eyes that I might see you. Turn me away from the path that leads to sin and destruction. Help me walk toward you. Grow my roots deep in your Word, that I might stand strong in you and be a source of blessing for others. And let me leave a legacy of your love and light everywhere I go.

Paws in His Presence

God's law is good; obeying him brings blessing.

The God Who Stays

How long, LORD? Will you forget me forever?
How long will you hide your face from me?
How long must I wrestle with my thoughts
and day after day have sorrow in my heart?
How long will my enemy triumph over me?
Look on me and answer, LORD my God.
Give light to my eyes, or I will sleep in death,
and my enemy will say, "I have overcome him,"
and my foes will rejoice when I fall.
But I trust in your unfailing love;
my heart rejoices in your salvation.
I will sing the LORD's praise,
for he has been good to me.

PSALM 13:1-6, NIV

Paws

The six-year-old dalmatian named Luca stood frozen in terror as Mary wrapped a large cone-shaped apparatus around his neck.

"I'm sorry, boy," Mary said soothingly, wishing she could make her dog understand the cone was for his own good. "We don't want you to scratch at your stitches and accidentally pull them out."

Mary knew neutering her dog was the right thing to do, but she hated seeing her beloved Luca so scared by the post-surgery cone the procedure necessitated. Mary sat next to Luca and patted her leg, an invitation for him to snuggle on her lap—one the affectionate dalmatian normally loved to accept. However, Luca remained rooted to the floor. Mary offered her dog a treat. Luca eyed the treat but made no effort to move toward it.

"Oh bud, I'm so sorry," Mary said. She pressed gently on Luca's side to get him to lie down. She cupped his face and planted a kiss on his black nose. "I'm still here. I know you can't see me as well, but I'm still here."

Luca sighed and eventually fell asleep. But when he woke up with the cone still around his neck, he panicked and ran frantically from room to room. Mary's heart broke for her dog, who couldn't possibly understand why his world looked different; why nothing felt familiar; and who surely felt abandoned and unseen. With his obstructed vision, all Luca could see was darkness and isolation.

"Luca, come," Mary called, shaking a box of treats.

This time he did respond, grabbing and swallowing the treat in one gulp. Mary pressed her face to Luca's face.

"I'm still here," she repeated. "I know things feel scary, but you are not alone. I am with you."

The words came from Mary's mouth, but she felt like God was also whispering them to her soul. Whispering words of hope into her own season of darkness and isolation as her desperate prayers seemed to go unanswered. She saw herself wearing a cone that obstructed her view of God.

Why aren't you listening? her heart cried out.

I am here, came a response from deep within her soul.

Why won't you intervene? she wept.

I am here, she heard again.

Luca licked her face, wiping away the tears Mary didn't realize she had shed.

Over the next few days, Luca adjusted to the cone. He even figured out that he could hold more toys in his mouth while wearing it. But even more important, he learned to run to Mary for reassurance that he was not alone.

Mary knows that Luca will never understand the *why* behind his need for the cone; but he has learned to trust the *who*—something Mary is working on too.

Ponder

Do you tend to freeze or frantically fret when circumstances make it hard to see and understand what God is doing or not doing? What circumstances are obstructing your view of God today? Are you in a season of darkness and isolation? How does knowing God is with you—that he is closer than your next breath—help you face your current circumstances? Take a moment to ask God to remind you that he is with you, even though you can't see him.

Lord, right now it is hard to see you, hard to know that you are with me. It feels like you have forgotten me, like you can't see me anymore. My thoughts spiral, and all I can see is darkness and sorrow. Lord, it feels like the darkness is winning—pulling me under, deeper and deeper. Please remind me of who you are; please let my soul hear you say, "I am here." You are my light, my hope, my salvation. Let me praise you once again, for I know that you are good. And whether I can see it or not, help me trust that you are always working for my good.

Paws in His Presence

God is always with me,
even when my circumstances make it hard to see clearly.

The God of Glory

Lift up your heads, you gates;
be lifted up, you ancient doors,
that the King of glory may come in.
Who is this King of glory?
The LORD strong and mighty,
the LORD mighty in battle.
Lift up your heads, you gates;
lift them up, you ancient doors,
that the King of glory may come in.
Who is he, this King of glory?
The LORD Almighty—
he is the King of glory.

PSALM 24:7-10, NIV

Paws

Early morning fog blanketed the field where Joy's six horses stood grazing. Their heads were cloaked in ribbons of mist as they pulled the tender blades of the new spring grass. The herd was utterly absorbed in grazing, yet the moment Joy opened the red metal gate, their heads raised from the mist, their ears flicked forward, and they walked toward the hay feeder as if summoned.

They arrived at the feeder before Joy. Dakota, a black-and-white pony—the youngest member of the herd—made her impatience known by pawing at the metal structure.

"Hold your . . . selves! I'm coming," Joy said with a chuckle, tossing hay into the feeder.

She took a handful of hay to her oldest and most gentle horse, Teddy, whose low status in the social hierarchy meant he was often last to eat.

"Here you go, sweet boy," she crooned, smiling as his velvety lips tickled her open palm.

She checked Teddy's hoof, grateful for how well his abscess had healed. Then she observed each of the other horses—looking at their feet, checking their skin for cuts, bites, and any signs of infections. Everyone appeared healthy, so Joy offered Teddy one more handful of hay before heading to the gate.

"I'll be back this afternoon!" she called out.

All six heads raised at the sound of her promise. Keeping six horses fed, healthy, and safe wasn't easy, but Joy couldn't imagine her life without them. Her horses had been her confidants, given her days structure and purpose, and when she started her own equine counseling and wellness ranch, they had even become her colleagues.

Joy finished the rest of her chores before driving to the local coffee shop for the first of four meetings. Securing funding for running the business was the least favorite part of her job—and took her far out of her comfort zone—but it was necessary. After spending the better part of five hours meeting in person over coffee, and then lunch, with potential investors and a friend who was helping her write a grant, and two hours at home talking on the phone with her financial planner and CPA, Joy headed back to the ranch—exhausted and distracted.

She longed to take a moment to pray and lay everything before God, and yet, her phone started dinging the moment she turned onto the driveway for the ranch. She responded to two texts from the woman helping her write a grant proposal, and two from prospective clients—a veteran with PTSD and a mother trying to find alternative therapies for her teenage daughter who was struggling with depression.

Joy tucked her phone into her back pocket as she got out of her truck and made a beeline to the feed room to get the horses' feed and supplements ready. The phone dinged again. And again.

I'll send a quick response and then get their dinner, she decided.

But one text led to an email and then to a message through social media and then . . .

CLANG!

Joy jumped at the sound of something banging into the gate. She peered around the corner of the feed room to find an annoyed Dakota standing at the gate, her front leg poised for another blow.

Usually, the sound of the gate would draw the horses to Joy, but this time it was Joy who was summoned by the sound.

"Sorry, pony!" Joy called out, gathering the rubber bowls.

Six hungry horses lined up at the gate, their heads bobbing in anticipation.

Joy set a bowl of feed in front of each one as she resurrendered her work and ministry to God, praying for the horses and the work they would do together.

And as the sun dipped below the tree line, she turned off her phone and committed to trust God with everything—even the black-and-white pony currently trying to steal everyone else's food.

Ponder

What does the phrase *King of glory* bring to your mind? How is the King of glory described in this passage? What are some ways that God has proved himself strong and mighty throughout Bible history? How has he proved himself strong and mighty to you personally? What are some things that tend to distract you from an awareness of God's presence? How might you lift up your head and open the gates of your heart to Jesus today?

PRAY

God Almighty, there is no one greater or more awesome than you. Lift my head to behold your glory. Help me open the gates of my heart and invite you in. You are the King of glory, and I ask you to come into my life and be my King. You are strong and mighty. You defeated sin and death, and I know that one day you will redeem and restore all things. Help me trust you, Lord. And keep my face toward you, almighty God—King of glory.

Paws in His Presence

Evidence of God's glory is all around me.

The God Who Brings Us Home

How lovely is your dwelling place,
Lord Almighty!
My soul yearns, even faints,
for the courts of the Lord;
my heart and my flesh cry out
for the living God.
Even the sparrow has found a home,
and the swallow a nest for herself,
where she may have her young—
a place near your altar,
Lord Almighty, my King and my God.
Blessed are those who dwell in your house;
they are ever praising you.

PSALM 84:1-4, NIV

Paws

Karen's heart had accepted the need to close a chapter of her life—leaving a position she'd held for years—even as her mind fought against it. *What if I'm making a mistake?* her mind demanded. *What will people think? What comes next?*

She had been working since the age of seventeen, and she never imagined she would be unemployed at fifty-eight. Yet, after months of sensing that God was leading her away from her current job—and after seeking wise counsel and spending countless hours in prayer—she had finally surrendered to his will and given her notice.

However, now as she entered her house, fear and doubt settled over her like a dense fog. She greeted her dogs, sorted the mail, and changed her clothes. She began pacing around the house reciting Scriptures in an effort to calm her fears. But after ten minutes, her efforts felt less like a spiritual discipline and more like a game of mental Whac-A-Mole. Karen inhaled a shaky breath.

"God, remind me who you are. Remind me of what is true."

Just then she saw her dog, Ruby, sound asleep on the sofa. The athletic auburn-colored bird dog was belly up, her back nestled against the soft cushions, her paws twitching with readiness to give chase at a moment's notice.

"Oh, my sweet Ruby," Karen sighed, gently rubbing her beloved dog's belly. "Home and safe, right where you belong."

"Thank you, Lord," Karen whispered for the thousandth time.

Although it had been four years since the horrible day when Ruby went missing, the memory still carried a pain Karen doubted would ever fully diminish. Needing to reassure herself that Ruby was indeed here and whole, Karen planted a kiss on her head. As she did, an image of Ruby tore through Karen's mind, effectively bringing all other thoughts to a crashing halt: Ruby lying in a neighbor's yard three days after she had run off and disappeared into the woods. The neighbor had immediately called Karen and helped the suffering animal. Karen had feared she would never see her beloved dog again, and yet there she was, alive, but so dehydrated and hurt from having been hit by a car, that she couldn't stand. It had taken a long surgery and many weeks for Ruby to heal, but she did heal. And she was home.

"Thank you, Lord," Karen repeated.

As the image faded, other memories flooded in.

Standing in the woods behind her house crying out, "Ruuuby!"; knocking on neighbors' doors; driving down dark country roads, willing her eyes to see her lost dog; calling animal shelters; posting "lost dog" flyers; begging God to provide protection, food, and shelter to the dog who had never missed a meal and who liked to sleep under blankets; pleading with God to bring her precious Ruby home.

Karen's throat burned with the memory of those prayers.

Prayers of desperation.

Prayers poured from a shattered heart.

Prayers uttered from the lips of a woman who had felt as lost as her dog.

Karen had feared she would never see Ruby again. And yet, during those dark days, she had never doubted God's sustaining presence. When all seemed hopeless, when she felt lost, God had held her through it all.

Ruby's back legs stretched out straight and she uttered a deep sigh of contentment. Ruby was home. Safe and secure and cared for.

"God, I don't know what my future holds," Karen prayed aloud. "And I have far more questions than answers. But I know you are holding me and sustaining me—just like you held and sustained me when Ruby was gone."

As Karen stroked her dog's velvety soft ears, the torrent of memories slowly began to recede. Karen resolved to step confidently into this new season. She didn't know what her future employment might look like, but she knew she was held by God, and that he was her home and her security.

And that was enough.

Ponder

What is your soul yearning for today? What situation has you feeling lost? Why do you think the psalmist longed to be in God's house? What blessings are found in God's presence?

PRAY

Lord Almighty, you are the deepest longing of my soul. Your perfect, beautiful presence is all I truly need. My heart and my flesh yearn to be near you—to see you, to dwell with you. You are my safe place, my stronghold. You are my home. Let me draw near to you and stay near you, all the days of my life.

Paws in His Presence

My true home is found in God's presence.

The God Who Cares

The LORD cares deeply
when his loved ones die.
O LORD, I am your servant;
yes, I am your servant, born into your household;
you have freed me from my chains.
I will offer you a sacrifice of thanksgiving
and call on the name of the LORD.
I will fulfill my vows to the LORD
in the presence of all his people—
in the house of the LORD
in the heart of Jerusalem.
Praise the LORD!

PSALM 116:15-19

Paws

"How am I ever going to get this all done?" Callie mumbled into her lukewarm coffee.

Her shoulders slumped under the weight of expectation—the expectations of others, but even more the expectations she put on herself.

When she was younger, she might have prayed about the anxiety and stress she had been feeling recently. But after praying—begging God—to heal her dad all those years ago, then losing him the weekend after prom, she had pretty much given up on the concept. She had decided that if God was real, then he was either too busy to notice her or he simply didn't care.

Callie's computer dinged with a new message—the meeting she was leading that afternoon had been moved to tomorrow. Grateful for more time to prepare, she refocused on the document before her.

BAM!

Callie's head jerked up at the sound of something hitting the kitchen window.

She walked over to investigate and gasped. The glass was fine, but there was a small bluebird lying on the deck below the window.

She ran outside and knelt beside the bird, unsure of what to do. "Please don't be dead," she whispered, trying to determine whether its rust-colored chest was moving.

A sudden and unexpected memory flashed through her mind of her dad gently lifting a sparrow from their driveway and placing it under a bush. "The poor little thing face-planted into the window and knocked himself out," he had explained to her. "He just needs a little time to heal." Callie, who couldn't have been more than seven or eight, had worried that a cat or snake might eat the bird. "Well, that's why we're here," her dad had said. "We'll watch over him while he heals, won't we?"

Tears streamed down Callie's cheeks as the memory faded. "We will, Dad," she said, sitting cross-legged a few feet from the bluebird, positioning herself so that her shadow shielded the bird from the intense sunrays.

Just a little time . . .

When several minutes passed without any movement, Callie decided to try something else she hadn't tried in many years—prayer.

"God, please let the bird be okay."

Something resembling peace enveloped her. She inhaled deeply, trying to savor the feeling. She studied the bird for any signs of life. The bluebird's wings remained still, legs bent, eyes closed. However, Callie was no longer seeing the bird. She was sitting beside her beloved dad—hearing echoes of her unanswered prayers. Whatever peace-like feeling had tried to take root was instantly shoved away by a familiar ache—loss mixed with hurt and a feeling of betrayal. "Why didn't you heal him?" she whispered to God, closing her eyes. "Where were you—where *are* you?"

A fluttering sound penetrated her mental spiral. The bluebird was trying to stand. It took several attempts, but the little bird finally stood on both legs. It looked straight at Callie.

"You made it! You're okay!"

Callie expected the bird to spread its wings and take flight, but instead it hopped forward—toward her. The small blue, orange, and white bird stopped about a foot from Callie and tilted its head.

"Hi," she whispered. As more tears fell, she realized she didn't know if she was talking to the bird, her dad—or God.

All Callie knew was that something profound had happened on that deck. Something had broken open and something had been repaired. And when the bluebird finally flew away, she wondered if maybe she just needed a little more time to heal too.

Ponder

Have you experienced a grief that shook your faith in God? Has your faith ever been shaken because of the death of someone you loved? Put their name in the following sentence and read it aloud: The Lord cares deeply that _____ died. What kind of chains might the psalmist be referring to? How might inviting God into your grief and pain free you from those chains? Why might offering thanks to God feel like a sacrifice? Have you ever praised God through tears? What was the result? What do you think might have broken open in Callie? What might have been repaired?

PRAY

God, I believe that you care deeply about our loved ones—and about our grief. I invite you into my grief. I trust you as Lord and King. I trust you, even when I don't understand your ways. Please free me from my chains of hurt, pain, anger, depression, anxiety, and doubt. Father, I offer you my thanksgiving, praise, and prayers—even as tears stream down my face and my heart breaks from grief. I thank you because you are good, even when circumstances are not. I praise you because you are sovereign. And I will continue to call out your name in prayer because you are my God.

Paws in His Presence

God cares about what breaks my heart,
and he is with me in my grief.

The God Who Forgives

Have mercy on me, O God,
according to your unfailing love;
according to your great compassion
blot out my transgressions.
Wash away all my iniquity
and cleanse me from my sin.
For I know my transgressions,
and my sin is always before me. . . .
Create in me a pure heart, O God,
and renew a steadfast spirit within me.
Do not cast me from your presence
or take your Holy Spirit from me.
Restore to me the joy of your salvation
and grant me a willing spirit, to sustain me.

PSALM 51:1-3, 10-12, NIV

Paws

The gray-and-black long-haired cat named Loki ran into the family room and looked at Rebecca. His head was twitching, and he was opening and closing his mouth in rapid succession.

"Did you lick off another knot?" Rebecca surmised.

Sure enough, a clump of gray fur was protruding from Loki's mouth. Rebecca took the furry knot from her cat's mouth and Loki responded with purrs of appreciation and grateful rubs.

Rebecca brushed Loki regularly, but no amount of grooming could keep up with the number of hair balls. Removing hair balls from Loki had become a normal part of her daily warm-weather routine as the cat's winter coat gave way to sleeker summer fur.

As she walked into the kitchen that morning, Rebecca remembered a very different routine when her family had first found Loki—a routine that involved trust building.

The former stray had been nothing but skin and bones, fleas and matted fur, and wary distrust when Rebecca's children found him living under a trailer stored at the back of their property. Rebecca's kids—delighted by the possibility of adding a new animal to their family—made it their mission to entice the pitiful animal closer to their house.

It had taken them a long time to earn the cat's trust, but eventually the cat began spending less time under the trailer and more time on the family's back deck. After several months, he even made friends with the family's orange tabby, Tabatha. Still, the wild nature remained strong in Loki, an instinct and skill he demonstrated by leaving various offerings of thanks at the back door for Rebecca and her family. Of course, that wasn't the only thing she would find at the back door. Hair balls often dotted the deck too. Over time, Loki began spending more time inside than outside.

One day, a year after Loki had been found, the cat was sitting in his favorite basket under the coffee table grooming himself when he grabbed and pulled out a knot. He began to lick frantically, trying to get the tangled fur off his tongue. Rebecca knelt down and gently took the offending clump from his mouth. After she did, Loki rubbed his head against Rebecca's knee. "You're welcome, Loki," she said. Rebecca was happy to help and assumed it was a one-time event. Yet a few days later, Loki came running to her once again in need of another fur-ball retrieval.

Now, not a week goes by in the late spring and early summer that Loki doesn't run to Rebecca with a clump of fur in his mouth. Rebecca is always happy to assist and grateful that her once stray cat has learned the benefits of asking for help.

Ponder

In what ways was Loki shown mercy? In what ways have you been shown mercy? Why is it important to confess our sin to God? The psalmist asks God to create in him a pure heart. What does a pure heart mean to you? In what ways does salvation—and God's mercy—restore joy?

God, you are loving, kind, and full of compassion. Please have mercy on me. Please forgive me for my sin—for the times I trusted myself and chose my own way over yours. I know I can't remove my sin; only you can. Please remove it and re-create my heart to want to honor and obey you. Keep me close to you and don't let me wander away, for there is nothing for me apart from you. Remove my sin, fill my heart with joy, and grant me strength to live for you.

Paws in His Presence

God is merciful and will forgive me of my sin.

The God Who Is Worthy of Praise

Let every created thing give praise to the LORD,
for he issued his command, and they came into being.
He set them in place forever and ever.
His decree will never be revoked.
Praise the LORD from the earth,
you creatures of the ocean depths,
fire and hail, snow and clouds,
wind and weather that obey him,
mountains and all hills,
fruit trees and all cedars,
wild animals and all livestock,
small scurrying animals and birds,
kings of the earth and all people,
rulers and judges of the earth,
young men and young women,
old men and children.
Let them all praise the name of the LORD.
For his name is very great;
his glory towers over the earth and heaven!

PSALM 148:5-13

Paws

Sweat glistened on Torrie's arms as she took a drink from her water bottle. While the mid-July Florida heat didn't seem to faze her kids, she felt like she was being baked in a humid oven.

They were visiting one of Torrie's favorite parks—a beautiful area of open space nestled along Tampa Bay, and yet she was having a hard time enjoying herself. The world was in the middle of a pandemic, tensions were high in their city, and anxiety had become her constant—albeit unwanted—companion.

She had hoped a visit to the park would be a nice distraction, but everyone seemed on edge.

Torrie was just about to call the kids over to leave when someone shouted, "Dolphins!"

"Let's go see," she said to her kids, leading them to the seawall. At least twenty other people had gathered there. Torrie had loved dolphins for as long as she could remember.

"Look, Mom!" Torrie's seven-year-old daughter, Skylar, exclaimed. "It's a mama dolphin and her baby!"

A chorus of *awws* rang out as the mother dolphin nudged her baby closer to the seawall—where admiring fans snapped photos and waved.

"This is so cool," Torrie's nine-year-old son, Jackson, exclaimed.

The dolphin duo swam along the seawall, picking up speed each time they passed. They zoomed back and forth and at one point the older dolphin turned sideways, giving her fan club a view of her pink belly.

"They look like my dogs when they get the zoomies and run around the house," a young woman observed.

"Aren't they something," an elderly man marveled.

"I've never seen anything like this before," said a man with the longest dreadlocks Torrie had ever seen.

Torrie observed the crowd of strangers-turned-dolphin-watchers. The group included a diverse mix of ages, skin colors, and ethnicities; some wore protective masks and others did not. Torrie had no doubt that the crowd represented vastly different political, spiritual, and ideological backgrounds.

But at that moment they were all united in their fascination and adoration of two bottlenose dolphins.

"I'm so glad God made dolphins, Mama," Skylar said, her face beaming with pure joy.

"Me too, sweet girl," Torrie agreed—a moment before getting splashed by the aquatic racers.

It felt so good to laugh with her kids.

A few minutes later, the dolphins swam out to deeper water, and the crowd dispersed. Yet, Torrie felt a twinge of hopefulness for the future. After all, if strangers could find common ground over dolphins, maybe there was more they could agree on

That night as her kids said their prayers and thanked God for making dolphins, Torrie couldn't help but anticipate the day that all of creation would be united in praise and worship of the maker of the dolphins—the Creator of all things. The good and faithful God who still held the whole world in his hands.

Ponder

When was the last time you stopped to praise God? Take a moment to consider what you know to be true of God. Reflect on what God has done throughout the Bible, throughout history, in your life. Consider making a list of some of God's attributes and the ways you have experienced him working in your life. As you offer praise to God, ask him to reveal anything you might need to surrender to him.

PRAY

God, you are the Creator of all things, and you are worthy of all praise. I praise you, my Creator and sovereign King. Thank you for who you are. Thank you for all you have done. There is so much that is wrong with the world, but God, you are good, and right, and holy—and one glorious day you will make all things right. As we await that day, set my face and my heart toward you. And please accept my humble gift of praise.

Paws in His Presence

No matter how difficult life becomes,
God remains faithful and good.

The God Who Shelters

Hear my cry, O God;
listen to my prayer.
From the ends of the earth I call to you,
I call as my heart grows faint;
lead me to the rock that is higher than I.
For you have been my refuge,
a strong tower against the foe.
I long to dwell in your tent forever
and take refuge in the shelter of your wings.

PSALM 61:1-4, NIV

Paws

The tiny kitten's body trembled. Her pitiful meow tore through Catherine's heart. She had found the poor thing shivering behind a dumpster at work—a common place for people to leave unwanted animals. Over the years her hair salon had helped rescue close to a dozen animals, often taking them to rescue organizations in the area. But there was something about the orange kitten that tugged at Catherine's heart and caused her to take the little male cat home. But now as the tiny animal cowered in his makeshift cardboard carrier, Catherine was second-guessing herself.

Woof!

Catherine's chocolate Lab, Daisy, came bounding into the kitchen. Her sleek tail beat an excited rhythm against the cream-colored cabinets. Catching the scent of an unfamiliar guest, the exuberant dog slid to a halt. She raised her head and her nostrils flared. The kitten, who had been shivering and making a series of pitiful wails, was completely still, pressed against a corner of the box. At seventy pounds, Daisy surely looked like a giant to the kitten, but Catherine hoped that seeing another animal might calm the frightened young cat.

"Easy, Daisy. Easy," Catherine commanded, lowering the box.

The Lab's ears draped over the edge of the box as she sniffed the kitten. And much to Catherine's surprise—and relief—the orange cat stood up and walked toward Daisy. The two nosed each other. Daisy play-bowed, but when the kitten scurried back to his corner, Daisy lay down and waited. After only a minute, the kitten walked back toward Daisy and meowed.

Catherine gently scooped the kitten out of the box and placed him beside her dog.

"Easy," she reminded Daisy again.

Daisy's eyes followed the little kitten as he sniffed her paws, rubbed his head against Daisy's nose, and then crawled over Daisy's front leg. Catherine couldn't help but smile as the little kitten crawled under her dog's floppy ear, curled into a ball, and closed his eyes. Daisy, seeming to sense the responsibility she had been given, lay perfectly still, and looked up at Catherine.

"Good girl, Daisy," Catherine softly praised. "You made our new friend feel safe."

Over the weeks and months that followed, the little kitten Catherine named Leo grew more confident and playful. But his favorite place to nap continued to be under Daisy's ear. It was a spot he went to often, and every time he did, Daisy welcomed her friend to rest under her Leo-sized ears.

Ponder

What is the cry of your heart today? Tell God—cry out to him; write it down; whisper it. Take your hurt, your hopes, and your fears to the God who hears you and who has the power to see you through the storm. After you pour out your heart to the One who loves you more than you can fathom, spend a few minutes imagining yourself tucked safely close to him. What do you feel as you picture yourself safely tucked within the presence of almighty God?

God, my heart cries out to you, please hear my prayer. I am at the end of myself—the end of my abilities and strength. Lead me—guide me—unto yourself, for you are my rock. You are above all. Father, you are my safe place, my refuge, my home. Remind my heart that I can trust you—even in this. You are a strong tower. My strong tower. Remind my heart and mind that I am safe with you. Envelop me in your presence. Hold me fast, forever with you. As the storms and stress of life surround me, hide me and keep me close to you. Safely tucked within your presence—trusting you, no matter what comes.

God is my safe place; I can run to him for help.

The God Who Remembers

Praise the LORD!
I will thank the LORD with all my heart
as I meet with his godly people.
How amazing are the deeds of the LORD!
All who delight in him should ponder them.
Everything he does reveals his glory and majesty.
His righteousness never fails.
He causes us to remember his wonderful works.
How gracious and merciful is our LORD!
He gives food to those who fear him;
he always remembers his covenant.

PSALM 111:1-5

Paws

After his wife's death, Arthur, a retired teacher and World War II army veteran, had been so lonely that he started spending most of his days outside by his garage, greeting people as they walked by. He would sit in a lawn chair, smile, and wish people a good day. Oftentimes, dog owners would be dragged over by their canine charges so they could greet Arthur.

As more and more dogs came by, Arthur had an idea. He bought giant boxes of Milk-Bones and set one out each morning next to two large bowls of water so he could give the dogs a snack when they came to say hello.

The dog owners appreciated the gesture. Some would stay for only a minute, others for half an hour or more. Arthur was so happy. He had people to talk to and dogs to spoil.

Year after year, Arthur's house became a destination spot for every schnauzer, spaniel, doodle, retriever, rottweiler, shepherd, and mutt in the neighborhood. As soon as they were within three or four houses of Arthur's place, they would start straining on their leashes. Sometimes, people would let go of the leashes and the dogs would bound ahead, across lawns and over a low hedge to get to Arthur, who would be waiting for them with a smile.

Eventually, people started bringing their lawn chairs and would sit and visit for an hour while their dogs relaxed under the shady oak tree in Arthur's front yard.

Every day, rain or shine, Arthur was out there—until one day, he wasn't.

Word slowly circulated around the neighborhood that Arthur was sick.

Then one day the dreaded news came: Arthur had passed away.

Over the next few weeks, the dog owners couldn't keep their dogs from turning up Arthur's driveway where they would stop, whine, and bark, wondering where their friend had gone.

When Arthur's adult children came to pack up his belongings and ready the house for sale, one of the dog owners had an idea. She reached out to all the other dog owners and planned a special memorial for Arthur.

The following Saturday, at 9 a.m., when Arthur's family arrived to take the last of his things away, forty-one dogs and their owners were waiting for them—lined up all the way down the block and across the street. The police had roped off the intersection so the dogs could safely cross the street to pay their respects to Arthur's family.

Arthur's children were overwhelmed. They knew their dad used to give the dogs in the neighborhood treats, but they had no idea how much he meant to everyone.

They got out the last box of Milk-Bones and filled the two giant dog bowls with water. One by one, all of Arthur's two- and four-legged friends walked up the driveway to pay their respects and say a final goodbye to their best friend's family.

Soon, Arthur's driveway and front lawn were filled with dogs and their owners.

That's when it happened.

A young beagle began to howl. His mournful cry was soon joined by others. The neighbors watched in awe as all the dogs in the neighborhood gave Arthur a forty-one-pup salute—barking and howling in unison.

"Thank you, Arthur!" the people cried, adding their voices to the tribute.

Arthur likely had no idea how much his neighbors—and their dogs—loved him. Even today, years later, neighbors still smile as they pass the house that a new family now occupies. The dogs still rush toward the driveway because to them, it will always be Arthur's house. And every once in a while, the vocal beagle howls.

Thank you, Arthur.

Ponder

What does this story stir in your heart? Have you known someone like Arthur? How did that person impact you? How might you thank them for the impact they've had on you? We are encouraged in Psalm 111:2 to remember God's amazing deeds. Why is it important for us to remember the awesome things God has done? How has God been merciful and gracious to you? How might you extend mercy and grace to someone today?

PRAY

Lord, I praise you and thank you for who you are, and I praise you for those who love you. Let me never forget or take for granted the great and marvelous things you have done. Let my heart and mind be captivated by your glory and your majesty every time I observe creation and consider what your hands have made. Let me remember your unfailing righteousness. Let me remember the wonderful works you have done in the past, and trust that you are still working—even today. Lord, because you have been so gracious and merciful to me, let me extend mercy and grace to others. I trust you to provide all I need; and I trust you to always keep your promises.

Paws in His Presence

God never forgets his promises;
he never forgets his people.

The God Who Speaks

The heavens declare the glory of God;
the skies proclaim the work of his hands.
Day after day they pour forth speech;
night after night they reveal knowledge.
They have no speech, they use no words;
no sound is heard from them.
Yet their voice goes out into all the earth,
their words to the ends of the world.

PSALM 19:1-4, NIV

Paws

Two hummingbirds darted back and forth between the branches of an old maple tree and the feeder holding bright red nectar on Janet's deck. The sound of their wings was slightly louder than those of the carpenter bees patrolling the deck railing, searching for a point of entry. A brilliant red cardinal perched atop a shepherd's hook as four gray, black, and white chickadees feasted on black sunflower seeds from the feeder hanging below. Hawks were soaring high above—their wings spread in surrender to the shifting air currents—while playful squirrels engaged in a death-defying game of chase, leaping across tree branches.

And yet Janet almost missed it all.

She had been so focused on the problems of the day, so fixated on her fears and lost in her worries that she had almost missed the beauty and life on display just outside her window. Instead of seeing what was, she was focused on what wasn't—and on what might be.

The only reason she looked up from her screen that day was because her dog, Stella, had started barking at something outside.

Janet's entire body had been hunched over—her head bent toward her screen; her shoulders slumped in surrender to her to-do list.

She jolted at Stella's piercing bark.

"Quiet, girl," she admonished.

But her four-year-old Lab/hound-mix continued barking—drool splattering the window as she kept staring at something in the distance.

Janet got up from her seat, her legs tingling from the sudden rush of blood flow. She looked out the window but couldn't see anything worth barking about.

Still Stella barked.

Janet scanned the yard for deer but saw no sign of the hoofed visitors her dog liked to chase. She looked for squirrels on the lawn. There was a pair playing tag in the trees, but Stella wasn't looking in their direction. Janet marveled at the heights the hawks were soaring. *Oh, how marvelous it must feel to soar high above the ground.* She smiled at birds congregating at their new feeder—a Christmas gift from her mother. And she was mesmerized when a red-throated hummingbird hovered at the window, staring at her as she stared at him.

Janet was so struck by the delicate bird that she didn't notice Stella had stopped barking. Instead, she rose and slipped quietly out the back door. Janet inhaled deeply, welcoming the scents of jasmine and freshly mown grass. She listened to the buzz of the hummingbird's wings. She lifted her face toward the sun and let the wind waft her hair away from her face. She closed her eyes and allowed the sounds of early summer to wash over her. And as she did, a hymn she hadn't sung since childhood filled her mind—and the chorus of "It Is Well" poured from her lips.

Janet will never know what Stella was barking at that day, but she will always be grateful she did—and for the peaceful moment that it brought.

Ponder

What is consuming your thoughts and attention today? Take a moment to look up and look out—look out a window or go outside and look at your surroundings. What do you see? Close your eyes a moment and describe what you hear. What do the heavens reveal about God? What is something you have learned about God through nature? Through animals? Spend a few minutes asking God to reveal himself to you in some way today.

PRAY

Lord God, the heavens declare your glory. The skies proclaim the work of your hand. Day after day they reveal things about you. Night after night the skies point to your majesty. Your glory, majesty, and power are visible throughout the earth. Please open our eyes, our minds, and our hearts to see you. Amen.

Paws in His Presence

God's handiwork is both small and grand,
both reflecting his glory.

The God Who Hears

The cords of death entangled me;
the torrents of destruction overwhelmed me.
The cords of the grave coiled around me;
the snares of death confronted me.
In my distress I called to the LORD;
I cried to my God for help.
From his temple he heard my voice;
my cry came before him, into his ears. . . .
He reached down from on high and took hold of me;
he drew me out of deep waters.

PSALM 18:4-6, 16, NIV

Paws

Anna had never felt more alone.

The weight of the past several months had taken a toll. She was at a breaking point, hiding in her room—desperate for someone to find her.

She could hear her family downstairs, laughing about something.

Did they notice her absence?

Did they even care?

Did anyone?

A wave of depression rushed over Anna. She dropped to her knees on her bedroom floor as the wave threatened to drag her under. She squeezed her eyes closed.

"God, I can't do this anymore. It's too hard, too much. If you're there, please help me."

Nothing.

Just the same hollow feeling. The same desperate fear.

The wave pulled her deeper. She leaned forward and rested her head on the floor. She wanted to cry, but her tears had dried up weeks ago.

Then something brushed her cheek. A cold nose. She shot up.

Her six-year-old boxer, Luna, and her eight-year-old pug, Winston, were both lying on the floor and pressed themselves against her. Winston on her right and Luna—whose nose she had felt—on her left.

Both animals looked up at her intently . . . expectantly.

"What are you two doing here?" Anna asked, rubbing each of their heads.

The two dogs had been downstairs begging for remnants of dinner when Anna had trudged upstairs, desperate for a brief escape from trying to hold it together.

It was getting harder and harder to pretend everything was fine. The truth was that nothing was fine.

Anna inhaled deeply and began to focus on the way Winston's breaths reverberated throughout his body. She noticed how Luna's ribs expanded with each breath she took. Anna ran her hands back and forth along each animal's back.

When Luna laid her head in Anna's lap and offered up her belly, Anna began giving her a brisk rub.

When the fawn-colored dog began to wiggle on her back to get Anna's hand to just the right spot, an unfamiliar sound escaped Anna's lips—a chuckle.

She obliged her canine comforter with a thorough rub in the requested spot.

As Anna sat between her two favorite animals, something inside her began to shift. Not in a dramatic way. In fact, it was barely noticeable at first. But it was there. A lightening of the burden she had been carrying around for months. With her pug snoring on her right and her boxer snuggled on her left, Anna felt—for the first time in a long time—wrapped in God's love.

She felt seen and known.

And she knew she had been heard.

She had asked God for help, and he'd sent her fur-covered helpers.

She inhaled deeply and whispered "thank you" to her slumbering companions—and to the God who had heard her.

Nothing about her circumstances changed as a result of their sudden appearance, yet something felt different.

She wasn't alone.

She didn't have to keep pretending everything was okay.

God had heard her.

And maybe it was time to let her family—and maybe even a counselor—hear her too.

Ponder

Do you think the psalmist was writing only of literal death and destruction in the psalm? What other types of things might the psalmist have been describing? In what ways do depression and anxiety sometimes feel like cords of death or torrents of destruction? Do you think God sent Anna's animals to help her? If so, in what ways did they help? Can you recall a time you cried out to God in your distress? How did he answer you? What deep waters do you need God to draw you out of today?

PRAY

Lord, my thoughts and emotions are in a tangled mess. Life feels hard and scary, and I don't feel secure. It seems as if the darkness is winning, and it feels like I am being pulled under the waves of doubt, fear, and anger. God, please help me. Please hear my cry. Let my words fill your ears. Reach down from on high and take hold of me. For if you don't, I will surely go under. Please lift me from the waves and save me. I need you. Send help and rescue me, Lord.

Paws in His Presence

I can cry out to God for help, and he will hear me.

The God Who Rescues

My eyes are ever on the LORD,
for only he will release my feet from the snare.
Turn to me and be gracious to me,
for I am lonely and afflicted.
Relieve the troubles of my heart
and free me from my anguish.
Look on my affliction and my distress
and take away all my sins. . . .
May integrity and uprightness protect me,
because my hope, LORD, is in you.

PSALM 25:15-18, 21, NIV

Paws

Elizabeth was glad to be home after running errands. She set down her bag and keys and looked for Blue, the family dog of about fourteen years. Blue's wagging tail, happy waddles, and a few short barks of hello were her standard welcome at the Czajkowskis' house.

Their beautiful Australian cattle dog with her multihued coat and two different colored eyes never shirked her duty as a self-appointed "official greeter." As a herding dog, Blue would often go a step further, pawing at the backs of Elizabeth's and her parents' heels until she'd effectively rounded them up in a circle right where she wanted them—together.

So when Blue didn't immediately run to the front door, Elizabeth was concerned.

"Blue! I'm home. Where are you, girl?"

The call was met with silence.

Trying not to assume worst-case scenarios, Elizabeth walked through the front room, kitchen, and family room, but there was no sign of Blue. Her heart beat faster, and she began racing to other rooms—the office and the dining room.

113

No Blue.

Elizabeth rushed upstairs. *Maybe Blue is napping on one of the beds,* she thought. That's when she heard quiet whimpering. When she rounded the corner into her bedroom, Elizabeth stopped in her tracks. She certainly had not expected to find the scene before her: There was Blue, three paws planted firmly on the ground, but her right back leg was caught in a knit blanket and stretched up behind her on top of the bed. Helpless and unable to move, Blue looked up at Elizabeth. The image might have been comical if not for the sorrowful expression on the poor dog's face.

Elizabeth immediately ran to her dog's side, knelt beside the bed, and began to untangle her. Blue began squirming, desperate to be free of the blanket holding her captive.

"Calm down, girl. It's okay. How did you manage to get stuck like this?"

At the sound of Elizabeth's voice, her dog settled down and she was able to carefully unwrap the blanket from Blue's leg. Minutes later, Blue was liberated from her yarn trap and leapt in delight. Any concerns Elizabeth had about Blue's leg possibly being injured vanished, as the dog bounced back to her happy self, launching into a quickstep with her little white paws and bestowing wet kisses on Elizabeth's cheek as if to say thank you. Relief washed over them both.

Soon after, Blue was back at her front window post, ready to greet Elizabeth's parents when they came home. Faithful, loyal Blue, always there for her humans and grateful they were there for her when she needed them too.

Ponder

What are some types of snares people find themselves in? Have you ever felt trapped in a snare? What emotions does feeling trapped bring up in you? In what ways does God free people from snares? How do integrity, uprightness, and hope in God protect you?

God, I need you. I'm watching for you. Please come quick and rescue me; release me from the snare that has trapped me. In your mercy and grace, turn your face toward me—for no one but you can help me. All I can see are my troubles. All I can think about is what's wrong. Please forgive my sin. Please take this darkness away. Protect me and help me follow you. You are my only hope, Lord.

Paws in His Presence

God is my rescuer; I can put my hope in him.

The God Who Satisfies

He makes springs pour water into the ravines;
it flows between the mountains.
They give water to all the beasts of the field;
the wild donkeys quench their thirst.
The birds of the sky nest by the waters;
they sing among the branches.
He waters the mountains from his upper chambers;
the land is satisfied by the fruit of his work. . . .
All creatures look to you
to give them their food at the proper time.
When you give it to them,
they gather it up;
when you open your hand,
they are satisfied with good things.

PSALM 104:10-13, 27-28, NIV

Paws

The sweet fragrance of jasmine greeted Judy as she stepped onto the brick pavers surrounding her screened porch. Two rabbits nibbled grass at the edge of her lawn, then scampered into the wooded area at the back of her property, while chattering squirrels leapt across pine branches in a high-flying game of chase.

Judy chuckled at their antics as she pulled the garden hose over to the pedestal birdbath sitting in the middle of her daylily and plumeria plants. She squeezed the handle and flushed out the old water before refilling the ceramic bowl. The simple act filled her heart with a soul-stirring joy. Her early retirement due to medical reasons and the pandemic had often left her feeling like the bottom had been ripped out from under her, but taking care of her animal friends gave her days purpose.

Judy had never really minded living alone, but at the time she felt isolated and forgotten. As one day morphed into another, her anxiety and feelings of loneliness began to swell. She longed for community. Longed for purpose. Longed for companionship.

One day, out of boredom—and a desire to try her hand at gardening—she planted a few flowering shrubs around her screened porch. Eventually, she noticed an increase in butterflies. Then songbirds began to appear. She bought a few bird feeders, then some birdhouses. She added more plants to the landscape. Now her yard was teeming with wildlife, and she took joy in providing food, water, and a safe habitat for all of them.

It didn't take long for Judy to finish refilling the birdbath. She returned to the house for a long-awaited cup of coffee, then took the steaming mug out to the porch. She sat on the swing her father had made decades earlier, and her heart swelled as warm memories wrapped around her.

Movement near the birdbath caught her eye. She expected to see a robin or maybe the bright red cardinal that stopped in for a bath several times a day. But instead, a large barn owl stared back at her.

Judy sat in stunned silence for several minutes as the large bird of prey sat in the middle of the birdbath. The oversize bird looked comical in such a small bowl, but he didn't seem the least bit bothered by the disproportionate size as he lowered his yellow beak to the water. Judy tried to get a photo of the beautiful owl, but he flew off when she reached for her phone.

Thankfully, two days later he was back in the birdbath, and Judy was able to snap a photo from inside the house. The following week she was refilling the birdbath when she noticed the owl perched in a tree.

"Well, hello there, buddy," she greeted.

The owl opened one eye, looked at her, then went back to his nap. She took several photos of the sleeping owl.

Day after day, the owl returned to the birdbath. And day after day, Judy would find herself looking forward to his visits. She also started sharing photos of the owl with her friends and family—who now text her for updates if several days pass without a new one.

Judy still lives alone, but she doesn't feel lonely anymore. She knows she has friends, both human and animal, who fill her life with joy and purpose—and who care for her just as much as she cares for them.

In what ways are God's fingerprints—his loving-kindness and care—evident in this story? How has God provided for you when you have been in need? What do these verses reveal about God's character? List some good things you have received from God's open hand. Who is someone you might be able to bless today from the good things God has given you?

PRAY

Sovereign Lord, thank you for all the ways you care for your creation. Thank you for the water that quenches thirst and nourishes the land. Thank you for filling the skies with birds who sing out in praise and acknowledgment of you. God, all who look to you are satisfied. All who trust in you have hope. Almighty God, from your righteous hand come blessing and goodness. Satisfy our souls with your love. Satisfy our souls with your holy presence.

Paws in His Presence

God satisfies my deepest needs.

The God of All Our Days

O God, you have taught me from my earliest childhood,
and I constantly tell others about the wonderful things you do.
Now that I am old and gray,
do not abandon me, O God.
Let me proclaim your power to this new generation,
your mighty miracles to all who come after me.
Your righteousness, O God, reaches to the highest heavens.
You have done such wonderful things.
Who can compare with you, O God?
You have allowed me to suffer much hardship,
but you will restore me to life again
and lift me up from the depths of the earth.
You will restore me to even greater honor
and comfort me once again.

PSALM 71:17-21

Paws

Phil and Bonne had endured a long two-month period without a dog. They had lost Tirna, their rescued Glen of Imaal terrier, to cancer, the eighth canine family member during their four decades of marriage. Now it was time to bring another one into their home. The couple had gone to animal adoption events and kept checking websites of area shelters, hoping to find a medium-sized, fairly low-maintenance older dog. They even mulled over the possibility of doing something radical: adopting a cat!

But when they filled out the application form for A.D.O.P.T. (Animals Deserving of Proper Treatment) Pet Shelter, they identified three possible matches from the list of available dogs. The initial two they met were wonderful. However, the first dog was far too big for Phil and Bonne to handle. The second was far too small. Thankfully, the third—much like Goldilocks's final choice— was just the right size.

"This is Darryl," Bonne heard the shelter volunteer say as he led what looked like a miniature husky into the room.

Darryl circled the room confidently, stopping momentarily to flick a kiss on Phil's hand, then on Bonne's.

"I love his little monster teeth," Bonne said, smiling at the crooked lower teeth jutting out every which way from his mouth.

"We don't have a lot of information about him," the handler explained. "Our best guess is he's a rat terrier/Chihuahua-mix, between ten and fourteen years old. He has a grade 3 heart murmur, but an animal cardiologist has already completed a thorough workup and written a detailed protocol for your vet."

"He seems to have a lot of energy," Phil said.

"Yes, he does. And personality," the handler confirmed. "He hasn't been here long, but he's become a favorite."

Having gone to the shelter specifically to give an older dog a good home full of love and attention, Phil and Bonne knew they had found their dog. They signed all the necessary paperwork, and the adventure began.

The black-and-white "pupper" took to his new home, his new family, and the cat next door with excited devotion. He loved his greyhound-sized bed and going for walks at St. James Farm, a former horse farm that was now a forest preserve. To him, it was St. Darryl's Farm, and he graciously allowed others to use it as a beautiful backdrop for photographs, especially with its narrow, arched bridge for picturesque poses.

Phil was retired, so during the week he and Darryl hung out together while Bonne was at the office. But like most every dog with an owner anywhere, Darryl knew when Bonne was coming home and never failed to greet her at the top of the stairs overlooking the foyer.

The moment he spotted her peeking around the front door, his big eyes got brighter. If she lingered and didn't immediately start up the stairs, he would give a few urgent "hurry up" barks. Then the elaborate choreography began. A spin to the left, a twirl to the right. Repeat. Before Bonne had a chance to pet him, Darryl was bounding across the living room as if he had flubber on his feet! Finally, Bonne convinced him to stop momentarily for a vigorous behind-the-ears rub, tender tom-tom taps on his ribs, and a quick kiss on the head.

"You sure know how to make a person feel welcomed," Bonne said, beaming.

The trio fell into a routine, which included taking Darryl for regular checkups. They were delighted when his most recent visit showed no significant change in his heart. However, the vet noted that the aging dog's spine was weakening. Phil and Bonne worried about his decline but resolved to give him the best care and make whatever time he had left with them as enjoyable and comfortable as possible.

When they arrived home from the vet hospital, Darryl insisted on running up the stairs on his own, as if to indicate, "I'm not over the hill yet." That night, as Phil and Bonne watched him snuggle into his bed, they knew that whether they had him for another two years, two months, or two days, they would treasure each and every moment together. They thanked God for the little dog with the murmuring heart who loudly proclaimed his love for them—and whom they loved right back.

Ponder

Would you ever consider adopting an older animal? Why or why not? The psalmist asks God not to abandon him in his old age. What might have led to this prayer? Have you ever felt cast aside or abandoned by others or by God? The psalmist exhorted himself to proclaim God's goodness to the next generation. How might doing so have encouraged his own spirit? Are you in a season of hardship? Talk to God about that. Ask him to restore and renew your soul. Ask him to ignite your imagination to consider the blessings and joy to come when you see him face to face one day.

PRAY

O God, you have been with me since childhood. You have been working in my life since I was born. There is so much I could tell others about you—so many wonderful things you have done. I'm getting older now, my body is starting to show its age, and I fear being cast aside. Quiet my fears, Lord. Keep me close to you. Focus my thoughts on you. Help me to proclaim your mighty power and righteousness to the next generation. You are so wonderful, and you have done so many marvelous things. Nothing can compare to you. And although you have allowed me to suffer hardships and heartbreaks, you

have been with me through each one. Remind me that one day you will redeem, re-
store, and renew everything. One day, you will make all things right. Give me strength
to wait in hope for that glorious day.

Paws in His Presence

From my first breath to my last, God is always with me.

The God Who Restores

When the LORD brought back his exiles to Jerusalem,
it was like a dream!
We were filled with laughter,
and we sang for joy.
And the other nations said,
"What amazing things the LORD has done for them."
Yes, the LORD has done amazing things for us!
What joy!
Restore our fortunes, LORD,
as streams renew the desert.
Those who plant in tears
will harvest with shouts of joy.
They weep as they go to plant their seed,
but they sing as they return with the harvest.

PSALM 126:1-6

Paws

Virtual instruction was not what Cassidy envisioned when she started her career as a kindergarten teacher. While working on her elementary education degree, she had pictured photos of the alphabet and handprint masterpieces dotting her classroom walls, colorful books on display in a cozy reading corner, and little chairs at little desks filled with little children.

For the first few years of teaching, that dream had been fulfilled—granted, with far more paperwork, teacher conferences, budget cuts, and sleepless nights than she could have imagined. But she honestly loved her job, and she really loved being with her students—all of which made the move to online learning during the pandemic especially hard for her.

She genuinely missed seeing her students in person. They had gotten into such a good rhythm after Christmas that Cassidy felt they would all be in good shape to move on to first grade in the fall. But then came the announcement. The school building was closed; and all instruction was moving online. Cassidy was crushed.

She knew most of the older teachers on her team assumed she would have an easier time transitioning to online teaching given her age and her generation's skill with technology, but the truth was, Cassidy felt as tech savvy as her cat, Pippa. She didn't have any social media apps on her phone, and it had taken her weeks to figure out the new grading software the school had switched to last year.

Thankfully, her cousin Trevor worked for a software company, and he had come over to get her home office set up. He brought her a webcam and separate microphone, spent two hours connecting everything, and even videoed himself turning everything on so she would be ready to go on Monday.

Although there were a few technical glitches, the first day of online learning went better than Cassidy anticipated. Because it was new, the kids were excited, which helped Cassidy feel a little excited too.

But two weeks into their experiment with online kindergarten, the excitement started to wane. The children struggled to pay attention. Cassidy struggled to make her lessons engaging. And Pippa struggled with Cassidy being home, but not giving the black cat her full attention. One Tuesday morning, while Cassidy was trying to teach a phonics lesson to twenty students in tiny virtual boxes on her screen, her cat, Pippa, pushed her way through the partially closed door and jumped up on her desk.

"Hey! There's a cat!" Aiden exclaimed.

"Ms. Reynolds has a real-life cat on her desk!" Scarlett shouted.

Suddenly, all of the boxes on the screen were filled with her students' beaming faces. Then the barrage of questions started.

"Is it a boy or a girl cat?"

"How old is she?"

"What does she eat?"

"Where does she go to the bathroom?"

"Does she have toys?"

Cassidy stroked her needy cat and smiled at the excited children, whose exuberant laughter felt like balm to Cassidy's heart. As she patiently answered their questions, Pippa moved from the desk to the back of Cassidy's chair and started pawing at her mom's ponytail. A moment later, the black cat had Cassidy's blue scrunchie between her teeth and was starting to pull it off. The children roared with laughter.

"Pippa's eating Ms. Reynolds's hair!"

After reaching around and extricating Pippa from her hair, Cassidy asked her students if they would like Pippa to stay for their phonics lesson.

"YES!" a chorus of voices sang out.

Cassidy held up a flashcard with the letters TH printed on it, then flipped it over to reveal the word THICK.

"Pippa has *thick* fur," she said, emphasizing the sound the *th* made.

"TH-ick," her students repeated in unison.

"Pippa's fur is *BL-ack*," Cassidy said, holding up another card.

"BL-ack," her class repeated.

The class added four more special reading sounds to their list that day, but more than that, they had fun—something that had been missing from their recent time together. Cassidy encouraged her students to bring their own pets—or favorite stuffed animal—the following day to a special virtual show-and-tell.

She knew they likely wouldn't get much work done—and they didn't. But they laughed a lot and got to know each other in a way they wouldn't have been able to in the classroom.

The children began looking forward to Pippa's appearance each day, and Cassidy found herself looking forward to finding creative ways to incorporate her cat into her lessons.

"Thanks for making a hard situation a little bit better," she told Pippa one evening, planting a kiss on her nose. "I might have to figure out how to bring you to the classroom with me when school reopens."

Pippa demonstrated her feelings about the idea by stretching around Cassidy's neck and grabbing the scrunchie from her hair.

Ponder

Have you ever been in a season of exile? What emotions did you experience in that season? How did God provide for you during that time? What does the phrase "those who plant in tears will harvest with shouts of joy" mean to you? What has brought you to tears recently? What has brought you joy?

PRAY

Lord, whether I am in a season of comfort and stability or uncertainty and exile, let me remember that you are with me. And help me trust that you will see me safely home—whether that is here on earth or in heaven with you. Let me live with such faith and hope that others will notice you and notice the joy I have in you. God, restore, renew, and redeem what is broken in my life. Renew me as streams renew the desert. I trust you to bring good from the hard situations. I trust that one day you will make all things right.

Paws in His Presence

One day God will restore my joy.

The God Who Calms

Be still before the LORD
and wait patiently for him;
do not fret when people succeed in their ways,
when they carry out their wicked schemes.
Refrain from anger and turn from wrath;
do not fret—it leads only to evil.
For those who are evil will be destroyed,
but those who hope in the LORD will inherit the land.
A little while, and the wicked will be no more;
though you look for them, they will not be found.
But the meek will inherit the land
and enjoy peace and prosperity.

PSALM 37:7-11, NIV

Paws

The black-and-brown shepherd-mix named Mia sprang from her nap and darted to the front window. The thick hair on the back of her neck bristled as she released a series of ear-piercing barks. Her rapid-fire high alerts reverberated around the normally peaceful living room as Mia paced frantically from window to window.

Natalie wasn't sure when or why her three-year-old dog had decided garbage trucks posed a clear and present danger, but the normally easygoing dog became hypervigilant on trash days—and downright angry when the trucks pulled up to their curb.

Natalie had tried everything she could think of to help Mia relax on trash day. She closed the drapes—Mia opened them with her snout. She bought a compression vest to help with her anxiety—it didn't. She tried taking her for walks when the trucks were out to show her there was nothing to fear—she dragged Natalie for half a block as she ran away from the mechanical beast.

No matter what Natalie tried, Mia's fear was stronger. And her fear was often very loud.

Yet, today, as the trash truck moved closer to the house, Natalie decided to try a different tactic with her anxious dog. Keeping her voice low and quiet, Natalie began to talk to Mia about what a good dog she was and how much she loved her. As she spoke, she knelt beside Mia, wrapped her arms around her dog, and held her close. Natalie's eardrums were throbbing from Mia's frantic barks, but she continued her monologue about Mia's best traits. When the truck pulled up at their house, Natalie pulled a treat out of her pocket and gave it to Mia, who was suddenly quiet. Mia eyed the truck, but she drooled for the treat.

Natalie rewarded her with several more treats while the truck emptied their bins and moved on to the neighbor's house.

Mia remained focused, but her attention wasn't on the object she feared. Now, she was more interested in the person who had stayed with her in her fear—and on the treats in her hand.

That day began a routine that would impact Natalie as much as her dog, as they would sit together and focus on each other instead of their fears.

And each week when the garbage truck was making its rounds and Natalie would speak truth—and feed treats—to her dog, she began to hear God whisper truth over her. Truths like *You are loved; you are not alone; you are not defined by your fear.* Truths that enabled them—both dog and woman—to be still and trust the one who loves them, and who is there with them in every storm and through every fear.

Ponder

What fears are you facing today? How do you respond to fear? Does your fear ever cause you to get loud? This psalm cautions us not to fret. How would you define fretting? In what ways might it lead to evil? What does it mean to hope in the Lord? How does placing our hope and trust in God help us to be still and wait patiently for him?

Father, I am prone to worry and fret, especially when it seems that evil is winning. Please still my heart and help me to trust you and wait patiently for you. Help me refrain from reacting in fear-based anger and wrath to the evil I see around me. Keep my eyes fixed on you so that I don't follow my fretting down a path that leads to sin. Give me eyes to see things as you do, and remind me that in the end it is not evil that will win, but you. Teach me to keep my hope in you and lead me into your peace and security.

Paws in His Presence

God can calm my anxious heart.

The God Who Offers
New Beginnings

Open for me the gates where the righteous enter,
and I will go in and thank the LORD.
These gates lead to the presence of the LORD,
and the godly enter there.
I thank you for answering my prayer
and giving me victory!
The stone that the builders rejected
has now become the cornerstone.
This is the LORD's doing,
and it is wonderful to see.
This is the day the LORD has made.
We will rejoice and be glad in it.

PSALM 118:19-24

Paws

Sherri stepped out onto the back porch and inhaled deeply. Heavy spring rains the night before had left behind an earthy scent. She looked out over the property their family had purchased a decade ago, their own little homestead ten miles away from a bustling city.

A bittersweet feeling washed over Sherri as she remembered the way her two sons, Max and Sorren, had run around the backyard that first afternoon when they moved in. "Free range boys," her husband, John, had said with a chuckle as the then eight- and ten-year-old brothers kicked soccer balls as hard as they could, raced each other, and talked about building goat pens and getting lots of big dogs to play with. John and Sherri had treasured every moment with their boys while they worked together to transform the neglected fields into places for a chicken coop, goat pens, a cow pasture, and a large barn. It had felt so good to create something together.

The boys' handiwork was evident all over their property, especially at the base of the porch steps where their handprints were preserved in cement. A familiar mix of joy and sorrow wrapped around Sherri's heart. She walked down the steps and put her hand on each of her sons' prints. She and John had just dropped Max off for his second year at West Point and were preparing to take Sorren to start his freshman year at college. *How did the years go by so fast?*

Sherri could not have been more proud of her sons. They were stepping out into the world—embracing the callings God had placed on their lives. It was everything she and John as parents had been working toward and preparing their sons for. And yet . . . she missed the old days. *Why did parenting have to involve such joy and grief?* She wouldn't change a thing, and yet, she missed her boys.

Baaa.

A loud and high-pitched bleat brought an instant smile to Sherri's lips. *The kid is coming!* She pulled on her rubber boots and ran toward the goat pen. Sure enough, Daisy was pacing, lying down, then popping back up and pacing again. Sherri knew from experience that Daisy's kid was about to be born. She ran to the barn to get a few supplies in case she needed to intervene, but Daisy was an experienced mom, and Sherri doubted she would need to do much.

She was right.

A few minutes later, Daisy was cleaning her newborn goat. Less than an hour after her arrival into the world, the baby goat was nursing. Sherri knew she would never get over the joy of witnessing a new life enter the world. Nor would she ever tire of the honor and responsibility she felt helping clean a little goat, providing a safe environment for newly hatched chicks, or helping deliver a calf. New life was everywhere—and it was good.

After getting Daisy and her kid situated in a barn stall, Sherri stood back and watched the pair. Daisy was a natural, standing patiently while her baby searched to find where mama's milk was. Sherri knew Daisy would give her kid all she needed to grow and thrive. One day soon the newborn goat would join the herd.

The baby goat's arrival reminded Sherri that life is full of new beginnings and that while joy and grief often intermingle, each day is a gift from God.

A gift that sometimes involves getting to snuggle a cuddly newborn goat, which is exactly what she did later that day.

When have you experienced joy and grief together? Are you in a season of a new beginning or a bittersweet ending? Why are we able to rejoice in the fact that God has made this day? How does knowing God is sovereign over today—and every day—help you face what is to come? What is making your heart glad today?

PRAY

God, I have so much to be thankful for, so many reasons to praise you. You are sovereign over all, and you provide for every one of my needs. Thank you for answering my prayers. Thank you for giving me victory—especially victory over sin and death. Jesus, you are the cornerstone of my life. You are life, and you are wonderful. I give this day to you. I acknowledge that this day is a gift from you, and I am so grateful that I get to live it in your presence. Help me keep my eyes and mind on you so that I might rejoice in your presence and be glad.

Paws in His Presence

This day is a gift from God, and he is with me in it.

The God Who Strengthens

Praise the LORD!
For he has heard my cry for mercy.
The LORD is my strength and shield.
I trust him with all my heart.
He helps me, and my heart is filled with joy.
I burst out in songs of thanksgiving.
The LORD gives his people strength.
He is a safe fortress for his anointed king.
Save your people!
Bless Israel, your special possession.
Lead them like a shepherd,
and carry them in your arms forever.

PSALM 28:6-9

Paws

Samantha fell into bed with a sigh. Her eight-year-old hound dog, Sage, circled and fluffed her dog bed, then plopped down, releasing her own weary sigh.

A moment later, a high-pitched bark from downstairs caused Samantha to burrow under the covers and pretend she didn't hear a thing. But when the single bark from their three-month-old puppy, Toby, escalated into a series of howls and cries as he made known his disdain for his crate, Samantha threw off the covers and went to check on the desperate puppy. She stomped downstairs, irritated that her three teenagers and husband were all out for the evening. As she took Toby outside, she remembered all the promises her family had made before bringing Toby home.

"You won't have to do anything, Mom," her teenagers had declared.

"We will do the heavy lifting," her husband, Trey, had assured.

I shouldn't have given in, she thought. But when the kids paired their pleas for a puppy with pictures of adorable fluff-balls up for adoption at a local shelter, she reluctantly agreed.

To her family's credit, they had seen to the eight-week-old shepherd/hound-mix's every need—at first. Toby's little paws had barely touched the floor the first week he was with them. But as Toby's energy level and play-bite tendencies increased, her teenagers' willingness to help began to decrease.

Then four weeks after bringing Toby home, while Trey was at a sales conference, Samantha's mom called in a panic because there was a beeping sound coming from the basement. Both of her parents had bad knees that prevented them from walking down the stairs. They needed her to come over and investigate.

Samantha had learned from experience that the quickest way to get back to her own to-do list was to drop everything, make the ten-minute drive over to her parents' house, and figure out a solution. She resented the inconvenience, as well as her parents' refusal to move into a smaller, more manageable house, but she hated disappointing them. So she swallowed her feelings and went over to help. Thankfully, the basement's smoke detector just needed a new battery.

When she returned home, Samantha found Toby climbing all over an annoyed-looking Sage. The rust-colored puppy was trying to chew Sage's ears, nip her toes, and jump on her back.

"Guys!" Samantha had bellowed from the bottom of the stairs. "Why is Toby out of his crate?"

"He was crying," her daughter Cami called out. "He wanted to play with Sage."

"If you let him out of the crate you have to watch him," Samantha yelled. "He's had an accident on the rug." Her eye caught a glistening puddle in the kitchen. "And the kitchen. You need to come clean this up."

"Can't!" Cami called back. "I'm leading a Zoom study session in two minutes."

Samantha's blood boiled, but she swallowed her anger and cleaned up the mess. She clipped a leash on Toby and took him outside. She didn't blame Sage when the older dog chose to stay inside.

The next few weeks followed a similar pattern with Samantha falling into bed each night exhausted from caring for a highly energetic puppy, shuttling three teenagers around, running back and forth to her parents' house, and trying to keep up with her husband's ever-changing work schedule. Sage would also flop onto her dog bed, clearly relieved to be free from being Toby's playmate and jungle gym.

"God, I can't keep this up," Samantha mumbled into her pillow one night. "Please show me how to survive this season."

Several days later, while Samantha was driving Sage back home after her yearly checkup at the vet, Trey called to tell her he was taking Toby and the kids to get ice cream.

Samantha looked at Sage in the rearview mirror and smiled. "Want to go to the park for a bit?"

Sage's tail thumped against the seat as they turned into the park near their home. Samantha and Sage spent the next hour walking along the wooded walking trails, sitting on a bench beside a creek, and chasing each other in an open field. Even though her body was tired from their impromptu outing, Samantha's mind felt calmer than it had in weeks.

"Thank you," she said, lifting her face toward the heavens. "I didn't know how much I needed today."

On the drive home, Samantha resolved to have an honest conversation with Trey and the kids about shouldering more responsibilities at home and with Toby; she prayed for wisdom to create healthy boundaries with her parents; and for strength to say no when she wasn't able to help. And then she rolled the windows down and sang along to her favorite worship song. She knew it wouldn't be an easy road, but she felt ready to face the challenge.

When they pulled into the driveway, Sage leapt from the car to find Toby. "We weren't gone that long, Sage. You missed him that much?" Samantha teased. She once again whispered, *Thank you*, then went to find her family and play with both her dogs.

Ponder

How has God shown you mercy recently? How did he show Samantha mercy in the story? When was the last time you burst into songs of thanksgiving and worship? Can you recall a time when God strengthened you? How did he do so? Are you in a difficult season right now? How is God leading you through this time? In what ways do you sense him carrying you?

God, thank you for hearing my cry for mercy and help. You are my strength and my shield. Help me to trust you with all my heart. I am filled with joy when I think about all the ways you help me—it makes me want to burst into songs of thanksgiving and worship. Because you are my fortress and my safe place, I know you will give me strength to face whatever comes. God, you are my shepherd. Lead me in the way I should go and carry me in your arms forever.

Paws in His Presence

God hears me when I cry out for help,
and he will give me strength.

The God Who Holds Us Fast

I cry aloud to the LORD;
I lift up my voice to the LORD for mercy.
I pour out before him my complaint;
before him I tell my trouble.
When my spirit grows faint within me,
it is you who watch over my way.
In the path where I walk
people have hidden a snare for me.
Look and see, there is no one at my right hand;
no one is concerned for me.
I have no refuge;
no one cares for my life.
I cry to you, LORD;
I say, "You are my refuge,
my portion in the land of the living."

PSALM 142:1-5, NIV

Paws

The last place Justine wanted to be was at a horse ranch. She wanted to be home hiding under her covers, not attending a horse-themed birthday party for her ten-year-old daughter's best friend. But since the party was all her horse-obsessed little girl had talked about for weeks, Justine did what she did best these days—shoved her feelings down, plastered a fake smile on her face, and pretended life was normal.

But the truth was, life was anything but normal.

The horse ranch owner—a friend who knew a little bit about what was going on with Justine's son—invited her to spend some quiet time on the far side of the ranch during the party.

Justine's daughter, Daphne, ran to join her friends near the round pen where three tables were set up for the party. *She looks so happy,* Justine thought, managing a slight but genuine smile. But a moment later the image of Daphne morphed into an image of her son at that age when he had been a carefree, happy kid. Justine's breath caught in her throat.

Those days felt so long ago.

Justine wandered over to a shaded part of the pasture and leaned on the top of the fence.

"God, where did it all go wrong?" she prayed aloud, even as she feared he had stopped listening.

Her son's transition to college had been awful. Within his first year, he had gone from a cheerful kid to an anxious and depressed young adult. He had undergone a thorough medical checkup and several blood tests that all ruled out physical causes or substance abuse concerns, so the theories shifted to some kind of mental illness.

Justine found a therapist, and then a psychiatrist. She drove her son to appointments, checked in with him regularly, and prayed for him constantly. She was hopeful medications would help, but they only seemed to make things worse.

Justine was terrified for her son—her sweet, tenderhearted son. He was sinking deeper into despair and hopelessness. And with five confirmed suicides at his college in the past year, Justine couldn't help but fear the worst.

"God, please . . . please help him. Help us," she pleaded, tears streaming down her cheeks. "I can't lose him. Oh God, please don't let me lose him."

Her breaths grew shallow. Her arms grew heavy, and her hands tingled.

"I can't carry this anymore."

Justine closed her eyes and rested her head on the rough wooden railing as she felt her own darkness beckon her deeper.

A sudden puff of warm air gently brushed the back of her neck. When she opened her eyes, there were two chestnut-colored legs with white socks in front of her.

"Hi, Samson," Justine mumbled, recognizing the white socks of the biggest horse in the small herd. "The party's over there." She half-heartedly pointed toward the round pen.

Samson—the leader and protector of the herd—leaned his head over the fence and exhaled.

"Not feeling the party vibe today either, huh?" Justine asked, reaching up to stroke his neck. "You can stay here and take a break with me."

Horse and woman exhaled in unison.

"It's hard taking care of your herd isn't it, buddy?"

A sob ricocheted through Justine's body as she spoke the words. The intensity of the emotional dam breaking left her shaking and grabbing for something solid.

Samson.

She wrapped her arms around the horse's neck and held tightly as two years' worth of fear, anxiety, and despair poured out of her.

"It hurts so much," she cried—whether to Samson, herself, or God, she didn't know. "Oh God . . . please. Help . . ."

Samson's head continued to rest on Justine and her hands held fast to his neck as herd leader and mother found comfort with each other.

Justine's sobs eventually stilled, and her breathing slowed. She released her grip, then pressed her forehead to Samson's muzzle.

"Thank you," she whispered to the horse—and to the God who had sent him.

Nothing really changed that day, and yet everything felt different. Justine left the ranch with a tangible reminder of what it looks like to hold fast to God and to have him hold fast to her. She would continue to seek the right help for her son. She would keep praying and listening and fighting for him. And she would do so knowing God was holding fast to her—and to her son.

Ponder

What lies heavy on your heart and mind today? Like Justine, are you trying to put on a happy face and pretend everything is fine? Would you be willing to take a few minutes to cry aloud to God and pour out your burdens to him? In what ways did God provide for Justine in this story? In what ways has he provided for you?

PRAY

God, I need you. In your mercy and grace, please hear the cry and lament of my heart. I lay my troubles before you—each and every one. I feel so weak, so broken, so scared. Please remind me who you are. Please encourage my heart. Lift my eyes to see you—

and help me remember that you are with me. Let your voice be louder than the lies of the evil one. Let your voice be louder than the taunts of my fear and despair. God, you are my refuge, and what I need most in this life. Help me to be aware of your presence and to trust your goodness and love for me.

Paws in His Presence

God will hold me fast through the storms
and heartaches of life.

The God Who Invites Us into His Presence

Better is one day in your courts
than a thousand elsewhere;
I would rather be a doorkeeper in the house of my God
than dwell in the tents of the wicked.
For the LORD God is a sun and shield;
the LORD bestows favor and honor;
no good thing does he withhold
from those whose walk is blameless.
LORD Almighty,
blessed is the one who trusts in you.

PSALM 84:10-12, NIV

Paws

"In or out, Henry?" Ellen asked, holding the back door open for her cat, who spent most of his time outside. "It's supposed to get pretty nasty out there today. Why don't you come in?"

Henry, a loving but fiercely independent feline, eyed the open door. He eyed Ellen. He turned around and curled up under the patio table.

"Suit yourself," Ellen sighed, walking back inside to start her workday, grateful she could work from home on such a stormy day.

At lunchtime, Ellen took a towel outside to help dry a soaked Henry. He meowed pitifully.

"Hey, it's not my fault. You could be warm and dry—and full of treats," she said, looking through the window at the new bag of cat treats she had picked up at the store.

She dried Henry as best she could, went back inside to eat a quick lunch, then reopened her laptop. Her computer dinged with an incoming message from her friend Nicole.

This video is so good! Made me think of you.

Praying for you today.

A link to a video popped up on her screen. Ellen sighed. She knew Nicole meant well, but her text stirred up something uncomfortable in Ellen's heart. *Why does she always have to bring God into everything?*

Ellen had grown up going to church. As a young girl she had even prayed a prayer asking Jesus to be the Lord over her life. But somewhere between her tumultuous teen years, her independent college years, a painful divorce, and two different careers, her spiritual life had all but fizzled. And it now mostly consisted of attending church services at Christmas and Easter. Ellen still believed God was real, but she had fallen into a comfortable rhythm of managing things on her own and hadn't really given God much thought.

Since her mom's cancer diagnosis, though, she had started thinking a little bit about heaven and even uttering a few prayers for her mom.

Ellen's finger hovered over the video Nicole had sent. She started to delete it, but something caused her to click on the video instead.

A woman's face filled her screen. She was standing on a round stage in front of a group of women. She stood confidently and spoke with a quick, engaging cadence. It was clear the woman was a dynamic speaker. And yet it wasn't how she was speaking that grabbed Ellen's attention—it was what she was saying.

She was talking about God's pursuit of his children, about his never-ending love, and his desire for his children to come to him—even if they've been gone for a long, long time. *Could it really be that easy? Would God really welcome her back?* Ellen replayed the video, trying to understand why she was having such a strong reaction to the woman's words.

Mrrow.

Henry peered in at Ellen through the kitchen window. The rain had started again, and the poor cat's drenched fur poked up in wet fuzzy spikes. He pawed at the window to come in.

Ellen grabbed a towel, then opened the door.

"Are you ready to come in now?" Henry looked up at her. He took a few steps forward, then stopped just outside of the doorway. "In or out, little one?"

The words came from her mouth yet landed in her heart. She might have been talking to the cat, but she suddenly felt like God was talking to her.

Ellen inhaled deeply.

"I think I want to come in," she whispered, feeling herself begin to surrender to a divine invitation—an invitation to draw closer to God and get to know him all over again.

As Ellen let herself take a small step toward God, Henry stepped over the threshold and into the warmth of his home.

Ponder

How would you paraphrase the first four lines of this psalm? When was the last time you felt an awareness of being in God's presence? Why do we sometimes reject God's invitation to draw near? Read all of Psalm 84. What blessings can be found when we draw near to God?

PRAY

Lord, I would rather spend one day with you than a thousand without you. You are where I find true acceptance and belonging. Forgive me for looking elsewhere to find what only you can give. Lord, you give light and life and strength. In you are blessings and honor, and from your hand comes mercy and grace in abundance. You are the almighty God—and those who trust in you are blessed.

Paws in His Presence

Abundant blessings are found in God's presence.

36

The God Who Satisfies
Our Heart's Desires

Trust in the LORD and do good.
Then you will live safely in the land and prosper.
Take delight in the LORD,
and he will give you your heart's desires.
Commit everything you do to the LORD.
Trust him, and he will help you.

PSALM 37:3-5

Paws

It was an exciting day when Patrick and Danika finally met the English bulldog who lived a few houses down from Danika's house. Patrick had always been an animal lover, and after two-and-a-half years of dating, Danika had become almost as enthusiastic as he was when they saw a dog. The two of them agreed that bulldogs were among the cutest canines, so when they saw one of Danika's neighbors walking an English bulldog in her neighborhood, they crossed the street to say hello. Brody licked Danika's and Patrick's hands, sniffed their legs, and wiggled his entire back end in greeting. His owner, Amy, introduced herself and Brody. The couple were smitten with Brody's affection and attitude and Amy's warm graciousness.

"Maybe someday we'll have a bulldog of our own," Patrick said, as they continued their walk.

Someday we'll have . . . The words stuck in Danika's mind. *Is Patrick getting serious?* She had fallen in love with him early in their relationship and believed he was the one. Maybe he was thinking that way about her. She had begun praying in earnest for their future and surrendering her plans and dreams to God.

As spring turned into summer, they saw more and more of Brody and Amy,

157

and even joined them on several walks. Each time Brody saw the couple, his entire body would wiggle, and he would give them nonstop kisses.

One perfect summer evening in mid-July, Patrick texted Danika to say he had a surprise for her. It was the day before her birthday, so she figured it must have something to do with that. The possibility of a proposal lingered in the back of her mind. *But probably not . . .* , she told herself. It was definitely just going to be a birthday surprise.

Still, Danika was nervous when Patrick arrived at the house she shared with her roommates. "Where are we going?"

"Just for a walk," Patrick replied. As they headed out the door, Danika was confused—they were going the opposite direction from their usual route. She peppered him with questions, all of which went unanswered—until they arrived at the neighbor's doorstep three houses down. Amy answered the door . . . with Brody beside her.

"We're going to take Brody for a walk!" Patrick announced.

Danika was thrilled at the opportunity to spend time with the bulldog. "Great! This should be fun. We can take turns holding the leash."

Amy cautioned them that Brody had already been on his usual evening walk and might be a little confused. How true it was. Getting Brody to move was the first challenge, and once they were underway, he kept turning to see where Amy was. The bulldog's bewilderment intensified in various ways—he'd stop to gnaw on tree trunks and licked Patrick uncontrollably when he bent down to pet him. The walk was just around the block, but it took Brody twenty minutes to go that far.

Finally, as they headed down the last stretch of sidewalk, Brody saw his house. As if a switch had been flipped, his reluctance was replaced with an urgent desire to reach his front door. He started pulling full force on the leash and Danika nearly fell down. A minute later, they were in front of Brody's house. And then . . .

Patrick was down on one knee—with an open ring box in his hand! "Danika, will you marry me? And share your life with me—a life that might one day include us walking our very own dog?"

Brody was pulling her as hard as he could in the opposite direction. With her arm outstretched behind the bulldog and only one foot firmly on the ground,

Danika managed to give an enthusiastic "Yes!" before Brody dragged her up the stairs and she stumbled to the doorbell. Amy answered, Brody slipped inside, and all was well.

Actually . . . more than well in Danika's mind. Patrick whispered thanks to Amy for lending him Brody for the momentous occasion. As the newly engaged couple walked hand in hand to Danika's house, they began talking about their future and started brainstorming possible bulldog names.

Ponder

What is the desire of your heart? What does it mean to "take delight in the LORD"? How might delighting in the Lord lead you to receive your heart's desire? What do you need to commit to God today? What do you need to entrust to his care—to his will?

PRAY

Lord, I want to trust you. Please help me to trust your love for me. Help me trust your goodness and your will. Then, from the overflow of that trust, let me do good—to honor you and to help others. God, let me find my delight in you. Have your way in my heart and mind so that I desire what you desire. And grant me the strength to commit every-thing I do to you. Help me to trust you, Lord, and help me live my life for you.

Paws in His Presence

God can satisfy the deepest longing and desire of my heart.

The God of Refuge

Those who live in the shelter of the Most High
will find rest in the shadow of the Almighty.
This I declare about the LORD:
He alone is my refuge, my place of safety;
he is my God, and I trust him.
For he will rescue you from every trap
and protect you from deadly disease.
He will cover you with his feathers.
He will shelter you with his wings.
His faithful promises are your armor and protection.
Do not be afraid of the terrors of the night,
nor the arrow that flies in the day.
Do not dread the disease that stalks in darkness,
nor the disaster that strikes at midday.

PSALM 91:1-6

Paws

Six fuzzy, yellow goslings explored a grassy area between a lake and paved walkway while the adult goose and gander watched from a distance. Storm clouds were rolling in, but the threat of rain didn't deter three families with kids from tossing bits of bread to the eager crowd of geese. The hungry waterfowls jockeyed noisily for the best position, delighting the youngest children.

While most of the geese honked for bread, a few napped in thickets or drifted lazily near the water's edge.

On the far side of the lake, a group of goslings were receiving a swimming lesson—following close behind mom and dad as they paddled out several yards before turning back.

But the six little goslings near the paved walkway seemed far more interested in pine straw than swimming. They stuck their tiny beaks between pine needles.

They poked their heads into bushes and hopped over dandelions. But when a clap of thunder signaled the arrival of the summer storm, the tiny explorers went running to their mother. She was sitting near a scraggly bush and lifted her wings to receive them. Six fluffy bodies burrowed under her beige wings until they were almost invisible to passersby. Every few minutes a curious gosling would poke its head through his mother's protective feathers, only to retreat back to the dry warmth of her wings when raindrops pelted him.

The summer storm left as quickly as it came, and one by one, the goslings emerged from under their mother's wings and set off once again to investigate their surroundings. They hopped and waddled, whistled and chased, pecked and played. Yet every time something startled them—whether a bike whizzing by, an overly excited child, or a loud wagon being pulled on the walkway—their mother immediately would raise her wings and the goslings would scramble under until the danger had passed. Day after day, as the goslings sought shelter in her wings, they would emerge a little more confident about facing their next adventure. Confident that she would be their refuge, guarding them and strengthening them to be a refuge for their own goslings someday.

Ponder

What does it mean to you to find rest in the shadow of the Almighty? Where, or to whom, do you run when the storms of life rage? What feels frightening to you today? In what ways do God's promises protect us? Will you ask God to hide you in the shelter of his wings? And while you're there, will you tell him everything that is causing you fear and stress?

PRAY

Father, I want to live in the shelter of your presence and find rest in the shadow of your love. You are my refuge and the place where I am safe. You are God and I trust you. There are so many things that feel threatening to me—so many fears and anxieties. It is so easy to become overwhelmed. Please cover me with your feathers and shelter me under your wings. Let your faithful promises be my armor and protection—may they guard me from my anxious thoughts at night and from temptations that bombard me during the day. Be my strength, Lord. Steady my heart and keep me close to you—for in you, I am safe.

—————— Paws in His Presence ——————

God is my refuge; I am safe in his presence.

The God Who Helps

God is our refuge and strength,
an ever-present help in trouble.
Therefore we will not fear, though the earth give way
and the mountains fall into the heart of the sea,
though its waters roar and foam
and the mountains quake with their surging.
There is a river whose streams make glad the city of God,
the holy place where the Most High dwells.
God is within her, she will not fall;
God will help her at break of day.

PSALM 46:1-5, NIV

Paws

Jenna's insides trembled as she stared at her house from the front seat of her car.

"I can't do it," she muttered.

Silent tears gave way to body-shaking sobs as Jenna imagined walking into the house without her beloved dog, Bailey, there to greet her.

Bailey.

It had only been three days since their six-year-old Golden had died from complications after surgery for a bowel obstruction. It had taken days to accurately diagnose the obstruction—days which resulted in damage too extensive and severe to properly repair. Jenna had rushed to the animal hospital with her husband and two young children to spend a few final minutes with their precious Bailey. It was the hardest goodbye she had ever said.

The next two days were a blur of tears, anger, and disorientation as reminders of Bailey's presence—blonde fur scattered around like tumbleweeds, her favorite ball, the imagined sound of her tail thumping the wall—remained in the house.

Desperate for a reprieve from grief, her children had been eager for the school week to begin. So now, sitting in her driveway, Jenna was faced with entering an empty—and painfully quiet—house. She took two steps from her car and faltered.

"God, why?" she asked for the hundredth time. "Why didn't you save her? Why did you let this happen?"

Silence.

She took two more steps. Her heart pounded, and her breaths became shallow pants. She knew that the moment she opened the door, grief would hit like a tidal wave. She tried to steady herself for the surge.

Meow.

The stray cat her kids had been feeding the past several months walked into the garage. He rubbed against Jenna's legs until she bent down to say hello. They had all been surprised by the way Bailey had handled the presence of a cat on the deck. A surprised bark and a few curious sniffs were all the Golden had needed to make friends with the gray cat they all referred to simply as Kitty. Within weeks the two were greeting each other every morning and lying together in the sun. A fresh round of tears wet Jenna's cheeks. She stood up, resigned to the new reality she faced. Kitty walked to the door leading into the house.

"Do you want to come in?" The cat had never shown any interest in entering the house before this moment.

Meow.

Jenna opened the door, took a deep breath, and followed the cat inside her house. His gentle purring was a welcome distraction from the deafening silence of grief. Kitty kept step with Jenna as they went into the family room.

"That was Bailey's favorite place to nap," Jenna pointed out. "And that was her favorite ball."

Kitty sniffed the ball, then rubbed his head against Jenna's legs.

He followed her to the kitchen.

"She used to sit right here when I cooked, waiting for me to drop something—which I always made sure to do."

She smiled at the memory.

Jenna spent the next ten minutes showing Kitty all of Bailey's favorite spots before sitting down beside him. He immediately curled up next to Jenna's leg and purred even louder.

"Thank you for coming in with me," she said, rubbing his head. "You were a good friend to Bailey—and you've been a really good friend to me too."

Kitty continued to escort Jenna into the house for the next eight years, becoming not just a good friend, but a beloved member of the family.

Ponder

What trouble are you facing today? What fear is gripping your heart? Consider making a list of those troubles and fears and setting them before God. Then take a moment to reflect on the ways God provided refuge and strength for you in the past. Lean into your awareness of God's presence with you. Cry out to him—ask him to steady and strengthen your heart. Consider the following breath prayer:

Inhale—*God is with me.*

Exhale—*God will help me.*

PRAY

God, you are my refuge and strength, an ever-present help in trouble. You are with me through all things—through the highs and lows of life, through every storm, through the brightest day and the darkest night, and when my heart is overwhelmed. No matter what happens, you are still sovereign and holy and good, and you love me. God, remind my soul that you are with me. Remind my heart that I am held in your hands. I lay my troubles, fears, and anxieties at your feet and trust you to help me.

Paws in His Presence

God is my refuge and strength;
he is always with me and will help me.

The God Who Provides

The eyes of all look to you in hope;
you give them their food as they need it.
When you open your hand,
you satisfy the hunger and thirst of every living thing.
The LORD is righteous in everything he does;
he is filled with kindness.
The LORD is close to all who call on him,
yes, to all who call on him in truth.
He grants the desires of those who fear him;
he hears their cries for help and rescues them.

PSALM 145:15-19

Paws

Andrew had never seen such malnourished animals before. It was his first day volunteering with a local dog rescue organization, and the condition of the new arrivals surprised him. He couldn't stop thinking about his own dog and how, at her healthy, average weight, she would look obese next to the dogs currently staring at him.

"These guys arrived last night," Kay, the volunteer he was shadowing, explained. "We don't have much information about them. Just that they were found in a rural area and are obviously in pretty bad shape."

Andrew's heart went out to the pitiful-looking dogs. They didn't look very old, but they clearly hadn't known much kindness or care in their short lives. Their hips and ribs were visible through their short coats, which were covered with weepy red sores. Some dogs cowered in the back of the kennel and two growled, while several others looked at him with a mixture of hope and fear.

Kay led Andrew into the room where they kept all the food and supplements for the animals housed throughout the property. She laid out seven bowls for their newest residents. Andrew expected her to fill each bowl to overflowing.

Those starving dogs deserved to eat as much as they wanted. But in the first bowls, Kay gave only a fraction of the amount Andrew fed his own dog that morning. *Didn't she see how thin they were? Didn't she care that they were starving?*

Seeming to sense Andrew's objections, Kay explained what she was doing as she finished filling the bowls with the same small amount.

"We have to be careful when feeding malnourished dogs. As strange as it might sound, feeding too much too quickly can cause just as much trouble as not giving them enough food." She added some supplement powders to each bowl. "We have to start at about 25 percent of what they normally should be eating and slowly increase it over the course of ten days or so. We feed them a high-calorie diet four times a day and then slowly increase the amount until they reach a healthy weight."

Andrew helped Kay distribute the bowls to the dogs. Most were eager to receive them, but a few held back—unsure and untrusting.

"It will take time to build up their strength. And even more time for them to trust us. But they will get there."

A brown-and-white dog approached Andrew. The malnourished dog's tail wagged ever so slightly as he sniffed Andrew's shoes.

"Is it okay if I pet him?" Andrew asked Kay, not wanting to do anything that would frighten the dog.

"Absolutely. Everything about that little guy's posture is asking you to be his friend."

Andrew knelt down beside the dog and rubbed the back of his neck—scratching the same spot his own dog loved so much.

"You're safe now," Andrew assured the dog, who leaned all of his weight against Andrew's leg. "And we will give you all the time you need to heal."

Ponder

What are you hoping to see God do today? What longing of your heart are you asking God to satisfy? What do you learn about the character and heart of God in this passage? How has God cared for you in the past?

PRAY

Lord, I look to you today with eyes of hope, and I trust you to give me what I need. I know that when you open your hand, you satisfy the hunger and thirst of every living thing. God, I believe that you are righteous in everything you do—even when I can't understand why you allow certain things. I believe that you are full of kindness and that you are close to all who call on you in truth. Sovereign Lord, I humbly ask that you grant the deepest need of my heart. Please hear my cry for help. I trust you to rescue me. Amen.

--- Paws in His Presence ---

God is kind, and he cares for me.

The God Who Remains

I still belong to you;
you hold my right hand.
You guide me with your counsel,
leading me to a glorious destiny.
Whom have I in heaven but you?
I desire you more than anything on earth.
My health may fail, and my spirit may grow weak,
but God remains the strength of my heart;
he is mine forever.

PSALM 73:23-26

Paws

Two horses stood together in a field. The older of the two—a thirty-year-old mahogany-colored gelding named PD—stood with one back hoof slightly raised in his classic "napping" pose, while his slightly younger and far more anxious friend, Woody, stood with his head next to PD's shoulder.

Brooklyn smiled at the pair, who were together more than they were apart. Two equine friends who found comfort and companionship in each other.

Woody—as anxious as PD was calm—often stuck with PD like a toddler clings to a security blanket. The older horse's gentle, unflappable temperament grounded and centered Woody better than any horse expert Brooklyn had ever consulted.

But the relationship wasn't all one-sided. Woody provided companionship for PD—whose quiet nature and physical limitations often excluded him from the larger herd. Although he was the eldest of the six horses at the ranch, PD was on the bottom of the herd hierarchy. None of that mattered to Woody. For Woody, PD was a safe place in what often felt to him like a scary, danger-filled world.

Brooklyn continued to watch the two as she filled the water trough. She couldn't help but notice how much thinner PD was. No matter how much she fed him, the elderly horse didn't gain weight. His left eye was cloudy. And chronic back and hip issues had necessitated PD's retirement from working as a therapy horse at the ranch she had founded years earlier.

Brooklyn swallowed a lump in her throat. She couldn't imagine the ranch or her life without PD. She and this horse had practically grown up together. As a young girl, she had learned to barrel race with him and had ridden him in community parades. In her teen years, he had been her confidant and closest friend. And as a young adult, feeling called by God to start a therapy and wellness program at her ranch, she had found PD to be her dependable partner and coworker.

Steady, loyal, gentle, patient PD.

PD walked to the water trough with Woody two steps behind.

"Hey, guys," Brooklyn said, stepping on the bottom fence rail to scratch PD's neck. She leaned further over the fence to reach Woody's neck.

PD lowered his head to the water and drank his fill. As water dribbled from PD's rubbery lips, Woody also lowered his head and drank.

Brooklyn gave PD one last scratch, then went to prepare the herd's dinner.

"God, thank you for those two," she prayed aloud. "Thank you for giving them to me and thank you for giving them each other."

After feeding the herd and tending to her evening chores, Brooklyn sat at a picnic table to catch her breath. A gust of wind rustled the leaves and blew her hair around her face. A storm was coming in from the east. Woody whinnied his displeasure. His ears flattened as thunder rumbled in the distance. As another gust of wind blew, Brooklyn looked up to find PD standing beside Woody, his chin resting on his friend's back.

The youngest horse in the herd, Dakota, took off running—her black-and-blonde mane flowing. The other horses soon followed. Brooklyn loved the sound of their hooves. She loved watching them have fun together. But her eyes misted with affection for the two oldest horses standing off to themselves. Two old friends weathering yet another storm—together.

Brooklyn didn't know the future. She didn't know how much time she had left with PD and Woody, but she treasured every moment. And she thanked God for friends—equine and human—willing to stand with each other through the storms of life.

Ponder

Who in your life came to mind as you read this story? Who in your life has helped point your heart to God? How has God guided you through a difficult situation recently? What does it mean for God to be the strength of your heart?

Pray

God, so many things change in life, yet you never do. You hold me fast, and you always will. You guide me with your counsel through your words. You have provided a way for me to be with you, and one day I will see you with my eyes. Help me remember that you are more important than anything—that you are my greatest treasure. I don't know what the future holds, I don't know how long I will have on this earth, but I know that you are with me. You are closer than my next breath. You are the strength of my heart, and you are mine forever.

Paws in His Presence

No matter what happens in life,
God remains with me and for me.

The God Who Listens

I love the LORD because he hears my voice
and my prayer for mercy.
Because he bends down to listen,
I will pray as long as I have breath!
Death wrapped its ropes around me;
the terrors of the grave overtook me.
I saw only trouble and sorrow.
Then I called on the name of the LORD:
"Please, LORD, save me!"
How kind the LORD is! How good he is!
So merciful, this God of ours!
The LORD protects those of childlike faith;
I was facing death, and he saved me.
Let my soul be at rest again,
for the LORD has been good to me.

PSALM 116:1-7

Paws

Eric walked into the animal shelter with a determination he hadn't felt in years—
if ever.

The woman behind the front counter smiled. "May I help you?"

"I need a dog," he said.

Eric could just as easily—and truthfully—have said, "I need a drink," or
"I need a new therapist," or "I have no clue what I need." But a yearning from
somewhere deep within him had zeroed in on a need for a dog.

"Okay. Just follow me," the woman said, leading Eric to the area where ken-
neled dogs of all shapes, sizes, and volumes clamored for his attention. Eric closed
his eyes. *What am I doing? A few weeks ago I was ready to end it all, and now I'm
picking out a dog?* An unwelcome, yet familiar feeling of hopelessness whispered,
You have no idea what you're doing. Leave. You can't handle a dog.

Eric shook his head against the taunting words. *God, help me*, his heart cried, even as his mind questioned if God heard or cared at all.

Over the past several years, Eric had tried a variety of therapies, medications, and treatments to fight the ever-present darkness and anxiety he faced. He had received one diagnosis after another, each one like a puzzle piece that sort of fit, but not completely. He had learned coping techniques and breathing exercises, but the darkness still found him. His thoughts still spiraled. His mind remained a battlefield.

A part of him longed to die.

A deeper part fought to live.

Eric opened his eyes. He didn't know what his future might bring, but he knew he needed a dog to be part of it.

He interacted with several of the dogs at the shelter. He inquired about adopting a few, but the ones he felt pulled to were all spoken for.

Then he came face to face with a yellow Lab-mix. "This one has just become available to adopt," the shelter worker said. The year-old dog's chocolate brown eyes seemed to hold wisdom far beyond the canine's years. Eric knew he had found his new best friend.

He named the dog JD, the initials of the drink he used to turn to in an effort to quiet the persistent battle in his mind. It didn't take long for Eric to realize that the drink didn't really help him at all—but he discovered that his dog did.

JD depended on Eric and gave his days purpose. He trusted Eric to feed him, walk him, and take care of him, and in return, the gentle but energetic dog cared for Eric.

Eric loved watching JD run and play and jump, and was captivated by his dog's zeal for life. And he was inspired by his dog's faithful, steady presence in his life—a presence that made Eric commit to working on his own mental health so that he could be fully present with JD.

JD grounded Eric with structure and routine, but he also brought fun and a spark of creativity. Eric decided to take pictures of his dog living his best life.

JD was the perfect subject, and Eric discovered a deep joy and talent for photography. Others began to notice Eric's talent, too, and eventually he found the courage to start his own photography business.

Eric has no doubts anymore that God heard each and every one of his pleas for help. He also firmly believes that God sent JD to him to become his best friend, his teacher, his muse, and his faithful companion. Eric knows he will always have to work at maintaining his mental health, but he also knows he doesn't have to do that alone. Not anymore. Not with God—and JD—beside him.

Ponder

What is the cry of your heart today? What is your prayer for mercy? Take a moment to consider the psalmist's image of God bending down to listen to you. How does that make you feel? Take a moment to talk to God. Cry out to him like a child would to a loving and good parent. Reread today's passage and let the truth that God hears you settle over your heart. God hears you. God cares about you. *God is with you.*

Pray

I love you, Lord. Thank you for hearing my voice and for not being indifferent to my prayers for mercy. Because you bend down to listen to me, I will pray and talk to you as long as I have breath! Lord, when it feels like death and darkness are pulling me into the pit of despair, when fear and anxiety tighten their grip on me, making it hard to breathe and to think clearly, help me remember to cry out to you. Remind me of who you are. Remind me that you are with me—even in the darkness. God, you are good and kind and full of mercy. Please save me from falling into the pit of hopelessness and despair. Let my heart always remember who you are. Grant me a childlike faith that trusts you to provide what I need when I need it. And let my soul find its true rest in you.

Paws in His Presence

God listens when I pray.

The God Who Draws Near

The nations are in chaos,
and their kingdoms crumble!
God's voice thunders,
and the earth melts!
The LORD of Heaven's Armies is here among us;
the God of Israel is our fortress. . . .
"Be still, and know that I am God!
I will be honored by every nation.
I will be honored throughout the world."
The LORD of Heaven's Armies is here among us;
the God of Israel is our fortress.

PSALM 46:6-7, 10-11

Paws

There was a sacred heaviness in the car as Jill and her husband, Ross, drove with their therapy dog, Mollie, to a nearby town reeling from a devastating act of pure evil. When the news first broke of the horrific shooting at an elementary school, Jill hadn't hesitated to offer whatever support she and her team of therapy dog volunteers could give. But now that they were mere minutes from meeting those who were grieving the precious children and adults who had lost their lives in a senseless act of violence, she wavered. *Who am I to try to minister to these people? Who am I to step into their grief and pain? God, how can we do this?* she lamented. She took a deep breath. *Lord, we have nothing to offer, but you—you who can reach through the darkness, evil, and grief. Reach others through us, love through us, bring your presence into this place through us.*

Ross pulled into a small parking lot and grabbed Jill's hand to pray. "God, let us be your hands and feet—and paws," he prayed aloud, squeezing Jill's hand and patting Mollie's head.

They stepped from the car and were hit with an eerie silence. A shiver went down Jill's back. *God, be near.*

Three other volunteer teams from the Canines for Christ therapy dog ministry met them outside the funeral home where they would be stationed. The air itself felt heavy with sorrow. The expressions on people's faces were a mixture of grief, shock, and disbelief. *God, be near.*

Jill led Mollie, their large Anatolian shepherd-mix, over to the other teams. They exchanged somber greetings before praying together and checking in with the staff. They divided into four teams—two would make themselves available outside and two would remain inside.

Zoey, a labradoodle, and Belle, a Labrador retriever, stood outside with their handlers and greeted those approaching the funeral home, while Henry, a goldendoodle, and Mollie remained inside. It amazed Jill when several young children came running up to pet Mollie and Henry. Their smiles were a stark contrast to the pained expressions on the adults' faces.

"Can I pet your dog?" a little girl asked.

"Of course," Jill answered. "This is Mollie. She loves meeting new friends."

"Hi, Mollie," the young girl said, giggling when Mollie raised her paw.

The little girl ran back to the couple whose red-rimmed eyes displayed their raw pain. Jill spent the next several minutes asking God to hold them and steady them through the day.

Minutes later, a group of children led a woman over to Henry and Mollie. Jill guessed the woman was their teacher. Her haunted eyes met Jill's for a brief moment before she turned her attention to the dogs. She ran her hand over Henry's head, then Mollie's. She kept her hand on Mollie's head as the children chattered about their own dogs. The woman didn't say a word, just wiped a steady stream of tears from her cheeks.

Several minutes later, the first little girl returned and tugged on Jill's shirt. "Can Mollie come inside with me?"

It took Jill a moment to realize the child wanted her and Ross to bring Mollie into the viewing room. Jill looked up at the girl's father, whose visible grief broke her heart. He nodded slightly. Ross led Mollie into the room, and the young girl took Jill's hand.

"That's my sister," she said, pointing to a small casket.

God, be near, Jill pleaded.

The precious girl stood beside Mollie—running her slender fingers through her fur—as Jill and Ross offered their deepest sympathies and prayers to her parents.

The family asked Jill and Ross to stay throughout the viewing. It was heartbreaking and yet beautiful to watch Mollie step into the inner sanctum of people's grief and offer God's love and presence.

That week, Jill and Ross and several other volunteer teams attended every funeral and memorial service. Over the next several weeks, they took their dogs to first responder stations and hospitals, prayed at the memorials, and did prayer walks around the site of the tragedy. And months later, when the new school year started, they began making weekly visits to the schools.

"We will be here as long as you need us," Jill had told a school administrator.

"I think we may always need you—you and your fur-covered angels of mercy," she said.

Jill, Ross, and the entire team of Canines for Christ volunteers prayed—along with the school administrators—about how they could best continue to serve the community. They began to formulate an idea about having a resident therapy dog, one who would always be available to the students.

A little while later their prayers were answered when a local family felt led to donate a dog to the school. Ministry volunteers offered to train the dog, and before long the students were introduced to their very own resident therapy dog, Kai—a sweet and gentle chocolate brown dog.

A constant canine companion and friend. A fur-covered confidant. A permanent reminder of God's love and sustaining presence with them.

Ponder

When was the last time you were deeply aware of God's presence with you? In what ways did the therapy dogs in this story reflect God's love and heart for the people? Why was Jill nervous in the beginning of the story? What did she continue to pray? How did God answer her? This psalm says, "Be still, and know that I am God!" What is keeping you from being still today? Will you take a few moments to quiet your body and mind and reflect on the character and heart of God?

PRAY

God, it feels like the world is in utter chaos and disarray. There is so much confusion, anger, evil, and greed that it becomes hard to remember you are here. But I know you are. You—the God of angel armies—are here with us. You—the God of Abraham, Isaac, and Jacob—are with me, in this very moment. Quiet my heart, Lord. Still my body and my mind that I might remember and be able to reflect on you. Remind me of who you are. Remind me of who I am in you. And remind me that one day, every nation and every person will honor and worship you. God, remind me that you are here, that you are with me, and that you are for me.

Paws in His Presence

God is near, even when he feels far away.

The God Who Protects

The LORD is my light and my salvation—
whom shall I fear?
The LORD is the stronghold of my life—
of whom shall I be afraid?
When the wicked advance against me
to devour me,
it is my enemies and my foes
who will stumble and fall.
Though an army besiege me,
my heart will not fear;
though war break out against me,
even then I will be confident.

PSALM 27:1-3, NIV

Paws

Nate walked outside with his five-year-old hound-mix, Ollie. While Ollie looked for the perfect spot to do his business, Nate tried to quiet his thoughts and pray. Why did everything have to feel so difficult? Work was stressful, his relationship with his girlfriend had hit a rough patch, money was tight, and the future didn't hold much promise of things changing.

Nate's prayer was interrupted by a bird dive-bombing his dog. Ollie—unused to an aerial attack—barked once, then ducked and ran back to Nate. Nate waved his arms, attempting to shoo the aggressive gray bird away. But the small bird wheeled around and squawked at him.

Nate led Ollie back into the house. *Can birds have rabies? What else would make this bird act so aggressively?* It didn't take long to find the answer. First, Nate scrolled through a bird identification app and found the angry bird's match—a mockingbird. Through the window, Nate watched the gray bird pick up a worm, fly to a nearby fern, and drop it into the open mouth of one of her fledglings before flying off to find another worm. Nate instantly forgave the bird's protective actions.

For the next two days, Nate enjoyed sitting and watching the avian parents protect, instruct, encourage, and feed their two fledglings. Nate even cheered to himself when one of the fledglings attempted to fly from the branch of a short shrub, then offered encouragement when the baby bird's attempts landed him back on the ground.

"Keep trying," Nate said out loud, remembering his pole-vaulting days in high school. "Every attempt makes you stronger. You can do it!"

Ollie sat perfectly still beside Nate as if he, too, was invested in the milestone occurring in their backyard.

A few moments later, a flutter of activity from the adult birds caused Nate and Ollie to stand up for a closer look.

Nate wondered if the juvenile birds were soon to take flight. But by the way the adult birds were swooping and squawking, it was clear something was wrong.

A snake!

A four-foot-long black snake was slithering toward the fledglings. Nate's mouth hung open when one of the adult birds flew down and began pecking the snake. And he laughed when the snake turned and slithered into the bushes. Yet, the birds barely had a chance to rest before a squirrel popped its head up from a tree branch and started crawling along the fence rail toward the fledglings. Immediately, there was a clamor of squawking, precision circling, and dive-bombing.

But this time the birds had help.

Ollie, who had been quiet through the snake encounter, started barking the moment he saw the squirrel. His piercing barks caused the squirrel to pivot and shimmy back down the fence, far away from the little fledglings. With the squirrel and snake gone, the adult birds set off in search of a meal for themselves and their fledglings.

The next day, Nate was delighted to watch the juvenile birds take flight with their parents. And later that evening, he smiled as mama mockingbird stood on the edge of the birdbath, while Ollie lay below it. Two animals so different in species and size. Yet, to Nate, both had become a picture of God's faithful care and protection—and a promise of peace to come.

Nate realized he might not know the future—and there was no doubt life was hard—but if two little birds could take such good care of their fledglings, he felt pretty confident God could take care of him.

Ponder

What fears are you facing today? What dangers are you asking God to run off? In what ways is God our light and salvation? What does it mean that he is our stronghold? How can we be confident even when dangers abound? How has God given you confidence in the past? Will you take a few moments and ask him to instill confidence in you once again?

PRAY

Lord, you are my light and my salvation. Because you love me, I need not fear. You are the stronghold of my life; and because of you I need not be afraid. You are more powerful than any fear, any enemy, and any sin that threatens me. People who seek to ruin me will have to face you—I can trust you and not be afraid. Even if war breaks out against me—from within or without—even then will I trust you and be confident.

Paws in His Presence

God is my light and my salvation;
he will guard my life.

The God Who Comforts

Sing the praises of the LORD, you his faithful people;
praise his holy name.
For his anger lasts only a moment,
but his favor lasts a lifetime;
weeping may stay for the night,
but rejoicing comes in the morning. . . .
Hear, LORD, and be merciful to me;
LORD, be my help.
You turned my wailing into dancing;
you removed my sackcloth and clothed me with joy,
that my heart may sing your praises and not be silent.
LORD my God, I will praise you forever.

PSALM 30:4-5, 10-12, NIV

Paws

Bethany couldn't wait to see Louie, her five-year-old French bulldog. The two had been virtually inseparable since Bethany had started working from home six months earlier. Bethany took Louie for walks twice a day and played with him in the backyard at lunch. Louie lay by Bethany's feet as she worked. And the gray-coated pooch had attended his fair share of Zoom meetings. Over the past six months, Louie had become more than just a pet. He had become Bethany's constant companion. And when Bethany went through a painful breakup, Louie had become her most trusted confidant—his soft fur catching every one of Bethany's tears.

Given how close the two had become, Bethany had hated to leave Louie for a four-day work conference. She had found a wonderful in-home pet sitter, and she knew Louie was in good hands. But she missed her dog. And by the photos the pet sitter was sending of Louie lying on what she had started referring to as the sofa of sadness, Bethany knew her dog missed her too.

191

Louie's brown eyes were so droopy and pitiful looking in the photos that Bethany didn't have the heart to tell the pet sitter that he technically wasn't allowed on the sofa. *I guess everyone needs a sofa of sadness*, Bethany reasoned.

Thankfully, the conference was finally over, and Bethany was moments away from being reunited with Louie. She entered quietly through the back door and tiptoed into the family room. Louie, expecting the pet sitter, barely glanced up. But when he did, he leapt from the sofa and bounded toward Bethany. She hugged her dog, then knelt beside him when he flopped over on the rug. Louie wriggled on his back—legs flailing and torso wriggling, pleading for rubs. A constant stream of happy noises erupted from him, seemingly coming from deep in his chest. Bethany had never heard her dog so vocal before. Louie chattered on and on, yipping, whimpering, and moaning joyful canine sounds.

"So . . . did you miss me?" Bethany asked, chuckling when her dog answered with a new round of canine chatter. "I missed you, too, boy."

Bethany pulled a brand-new tennis ball from her pocket and offered it to Louie. In one fluid motion, the little bulldog got to his feet and crouched in his ready position. Bethany threw the ball and he raced after it, then bounded back to Bethany, hoping for another toss.

"From the sofa of sadness to the rug of rejoicing," Bethany said, laughing.

Her closest confidant swiped his tongue across her cheek, then began a new round of happy dog sounds.

Ponder

When was the last time you were inspired to spontaneously sing praises to God? When was the last time you wept over something? Did you share your grief with someone? Or did you carry it by yourself? Do you find that things often feel worse at night? Why do you think that is? What is something that has helped in the past when you've experienced anxious or negative thoughts? Who is someone you trust that you could share those difficult moments with? Can you recall a time God turned your "wailing into dancing"?

Pray

My soul sings praises to you, Lord. I praise your holy name. I praise you—for you are just, righteous, and full of mercy. I praise you because you hold me through the storms and trials of life. Whether I am weeping or rejoicing, you are faithful and worthy of my eternal praise. Whether my heart weeps with sorrow, trembles with fear, or rejoices with singing, you are with me and you are for me, and for that—and so much more—God, I praise you.

Paws in His Presence

God can turn my weeping into rejoicing;
and he will hold me through it all.

The God Who Catches Us When We Fall

The LORD is good to everyone.
He showers compassion on all his creation.
All of your works will thank you, LORD,
and your faithful followers will praise you.
They will speak of the glory of your kingdom;
they will give examples of your power.
They will tell about your mighty deeds
and about the majesty and glory of your reign.
For your kingdom is an everlasting kingdom.
You rule throughout all generations.
The LORD always keeps his promises;
he is gracious in all he does.
The LORD helps the fallen
and lifts those bent beneath their loads.

PSALM 145:9-14

Paws

Tia's hand was about to knock, but she hesitated. *I shouldn't have come*, she thought, suddenly questioning her decision to attend a friend's book club.

"Just give it a try," her friend Shontell had suggested the week before. "We meet once a month to talk about what we're reading and suggest books to each other. It's really casual. I think it would be good for you to come."

At the time, Tia had appreciated her friend's concern. Shontell knew how difficult life had been for her since losing her husband to cancer four months earlier. His death had shaken Tia's entire world and left her feeling unsteady, unsure, and lonely.

Tia pulled her hand back to knock but couldn't bring herself to do it. *I don't want to be around a bunch of strangers*, she realized, dropping her arm back to her side. As she turned to leave, a deep throaty bark from inside the house startled her. Suddenly, the front door opened and a giant sand-colored dog came limping out. Tia tried her best to smile at the older man standing in the doorway.

"Hi! You must be Tia. I'm Ron, and that's Essie. She's been our greeter here for the past thirteen years." Ron's face shone with affection for his dog. "Come on, Essie." He clicked his tongue. "Let our new friend come inside and meet everyone."

With her plans for a quiet exit thwarted, Tia followed the two inside.

"Shontell told us you might be joining us tonight. We're glad to have you."

Tia followed Ron and Essie across a mismatched arrangement of area rugs and runners into a large family room. She figured the rugs were providing traction for the aging dog, who probably had a hard time on the tile floors. Tia took a fortifying breath and forced a smile to her lips while Ron introduced her to a group of six strangers. A moment later, Shontell walked into the room.

"Sorry I was late," she said, embracing Tia. "I'm so glad you came," she whispered.

Essie nosed Shontell's hand. "Hi, Queen Essie," Shontell said, petting the gentle dog. "How are those joints of yours holding up, sweet girl?" Essie leaned into Shontell but kept her large, round eyes focused on Tia. Her stare was both unnerving and inviting. Tia patted the dog's head, then took a seat beside Shontell on the plush gray sofa. Essie eased herself into a sitting position on the thick wool rug, her back pressed against Tia's legs.

"Looks like someone already found a friend," Shontell observed.

As each member of the group shared what they were reading and gave a brief summary of the book, Tia ran her fingers over Essie's soft ears.

When it came time for her to share what she was reading, she confessed, "I haven't been able to read much since my husband died."

Essie laid her head on Tia's lap and sighed. Tia stroked the dog's neck.

"Oh, honey, I could barely focus enough to read the mail after my mom died," said a woman whose name Tia couldn't remember.

"I couldn't stand to watch movies or see anyone happy for six months after losing my son," a woman named Becca added.

"After Nancy's first heart attack, I remember worrying that life would never feel normal or steady again," Ron confessed, squeezing his wife's hand.

Tia buried her fingers in the thick fur on Essie's neck and smiled. It felt so good to be around people who understood. She smiled at the group. "I would love some recommendations for when I feel like reading again."

Tia spent the next twenty minutes listening to a lively discussion about what she should read. At one point, Becca commented on a new carpet runner near the kitchen.

"Essie fell there last week on her way to her water bowl," Ron explained. "So Nancy went out the next day to buy another rug. We can't have our girl falling on the hard tile. As long as she's with us, she will always have a safe place to land."

A soft place to land. The words wrapped around Tia's heart. She scooted off the sofa to sit next to Essie and whispered, "Thank you for giving *me* a soft place to land tonight."

Ponder

What does the phrase "a soft place to land" mean to you? In the story, how did Essie (and God) provide such a place for Tia? Can you recall a time God provided a soft place for you to land during a painful season? How might you provide a safe, healing space for someone else? Psalm 145 speaks of God's compassion, grace, and power. How have you experienced these traits of God in your life?

PRAY

God, you are so good to us. You shower compassion on all your creation. All that you have made will bow before you and thank you. Your faithful followers will praise you. They will speak of the glory of your Kingdom and give examples of your power. They will tell about your mighty deeds and about the majesty and glory of your reign. Your Kingdom is an everlasting Kingdom, and you rule throughout all generations. Lord, thank you for always keeping your promises and for being gracious in all you do. And thank you for catching us when we fall and for lifting those bent beneath their loads.

Paws in His Presence

God is there to catch me when I fall.

The God Who Watches Over Us

The LORD himself watches over you!
The LORD stands beside you as your protective shade.
The sun will not harm you by day,
nor the moon at night.
The LORD keeps you from all harm
and watches over your life.
The LORD keeps watch over you as you come and go,
both now and forever.

PSALM 121:5-8

Paws

Willow, a black-and-beige bobtail cat, sat in front of the sliding glass doors and raised pleading eyes toward Keri.

Meow.

"We just came in from outside," Keri said. "You want to go back out already?"

Meow.

Keri grabbed a bottle of water from the fridge, then opened the sliding glass door.

"Okay, Potato," Keri said, using her favorite nickname for her feline companion, "you go explore, but let's stay away from the doodles' yard."

Most people considered the curly-haired goldendoodles next door to be two giant teddy bears, but Keri saw potential harm. The young dogs were overly exuberant and had a penchant for bolting from their unfenced yard. Keri knew that could be a dangerous combination should they set their attention on her petite cat. So every time Willow went outside, Keri made it her mission to stand between her Potato and the doodles' yard. She actually tried to anticipate any dangers that could possibly befall her adventurous little bobtail.

Anticipating danger is something Keri has done for as long as she can remember—a little "what-if" game her anxiety likes to play with her. Even though she knows and firmly believes that God is with her and that he cares for her, her anxiety still likes to play games of "what-if" and "imagine the worst-case scenario" with her mind.

"I wish I could be as carefree as you," she would often say as her cat climbed trees, chased butterflies, or bellycrawled to get closer to a rabbit.

Eventually, she realized that Willow was able to be carefree because Keri was watching over her. Sometimes that meant Keri had to steer her cat back into their yard or pick her up to avoid harm. If it was storming or the lawn had been sprayed, Keri wouldn't let her go outside at all. Thankfully, Willow seemed to understand that Keri had her best interest at heart and complied, even when it was clear she didn't like the situation.

One day, Keri's little Potato was outside exploring while she watered the plants on their deck. Keri kept an eagle eye on her kitty, and called to her as she started wandering closer to the doodles' yard.

"Willow, come back," she called out—just as the neighbors' back door opened and two very excited doodles dashed out.

They spotted Willow and leapt together from their deck. Keri, not wanting them to accidentally step on or scare her kitty, dropped the hose and managed to get to Willow in three giant strides. She scooped Willow into her arms and bolted inside the house. Willow didn't understand the potential danger, or why her mom was so upset, but she still hid under the bed out of an abundance of caution.

Keri worried that Willow would be too frightened to go in the backyard following the doodle scare. But thankfully the next day, Willow vocally requested that Keri let her outside.

Willow resumed her investigating, and Keri resumed her patrol. She smiled as her cat watched the birds at the feeder, followed a butterfly, and nibbled at a leaf. Willow trusted Keri to watch over her. And as Keri kept a close eye on her cat, she began to better understand that God was doing the same for her, and that he would be with her—even through the "what-ifs" of life.

Ponder

Would you describe yourself as carefree or anxious? What do you think has contributed to those traits in your life? In what ways does God keep us from harm? How might this passage apply to someone who is facing real danger and harm? How have you experienced God's protection? What anxieties and concerns are you facing today? Will you take a moment and talk to God about them?

PRAY

Lord, thank you for watching over me. Thank you for standing beside me as my protective shade and shield. Help me trust you to provide what I need, when I need it. Help me to lay my anxieties and concerns at your feet because I know you faithfully care for me. Guard my life, Lord, and guard the lives of those I love. Watch over us as we come and go—both now and forever. I pray this in your name, amen.

Paws in His Presence

God watches over his children.

The God Who Steadies

I prayed to the LORD, and he answered me.
He freed me from all my fears.
Those who look to him for help will be radiant with joy;
no shadow of shame will darken their faces.
In my desperation I prayed, and the LORD listened;
he saved me from all my troubles.
For the angel of the LORD is a guard;
he surrounds and defends all who fear him.
Taste and see that the LORD is good.
Oh, the joys of those who take refuge in him!

PSALM 34:4-8

Paws

The Australian shepherd's legs trembled as he walked.

"It's okay, Indy," Josh tried to soothe his dog. "Today is just a checkup to make sure you're healthy."

Indy pulled against his red leash in a desperate attempt to get back to the car. Josh urged his dog forward.

Indy whined.

Josh coaxed.

It was a slow procession, but they finally made it into the veterinary waiting room where Indy jumped onto a chair and sat with his back as straight as a board.

"I think they're going to figure out you're a dog," Josh said, laughing at his dog's attempt to disguise himself as a human.

Indy's entire body trembled as a tech led them back to an exam room. Josh couldn't imagine how much worse his dog's anxiety symptoms would have been without the prescribed medication he had given him that morning. Josh hated having to medicate his dog for vet visits, but given the severity of Indy's anxiety, the medication seemed like the kinder choice.

Prior to the medication, Indy would pant so hard the veterinarian couldn't hear his heart—something that was a very important part of his exam since the shepherd had a slight heart murmur. Indy also used to cry and yelp when the tech would take him into the back for tests and a nail trim.

Between medication and the staff allowing Indy to stay in the exam room with Josh rather than go to the back with the tech, things had gotten better. But even with all the accommodations, Indy still experienced a fear response every time he entered the vet's office. Thankfully, Indy had also developed a strong bond and trust in Josh over the years.

Indy had learned that Josh only wanted the best for him.

He realized that he could depend on Josh for food and water; he could trust Josh to be gentle; and he knew there was always a tasty reward for running back to Josh whenever he called, "Come."

So even though Indy's legs trembled as the vet looked in his ears, the black-and-white dog kept his gaze fixed on Josh.

"You're okay," Josh assured him, his eyes looking right back at his dog.

Indy's trusting gaze caused a swell of emotion inside of Josh. The weight of responsibility felt heavy—but it was a heaviness he would gladly carry for Indy.

When the vet needed to draw blood, a tech stood between Indy and Josh to help hold the dog's leg still. Indy began to pant. He tried to look over the tech's head. He struggled to peer around the tech.

"I'm here, boy," Josh said, moving so that his dog could see him. "I'm here and you're safe."

Indy's body stilled and his eyes focused on Josh—his safe place.

His refuge.

His friend.

As soon as they left the vet, Josh pulled a treat from his pocket and showered his dog with hugs and praise. Indy bounded from the vet with his tail wagging and his tongue hanging. He was now the picture of a happy dog.

Josh didn't know if his dog's anxiety about vet visits would ever lessen, but he vowed to be with him through each and every one—with treats in his pocket and ready to celebrate his dog's courage and trust.

Ponder

Can you recall a time you prayed desperately for something and God answered? If so, how did he answer? Did he answer in the way you thought he would? What are some fears you'd like God to free you from? How might looking to God for help give us joy? How might it free us from shame? Have you ever experienced God saving you from your troubles—even though your circumstances didn't change? If so, in what ways did he help you? What joys do you think people experience when they take refuge in God?

PRAY

Lord, thank you for hearing me when I pray. Thank you for answering my prayers. My heart holds so many fears, and yet I can have peace because you hold my heart—you hold me. Help me stay focused on you. Keep me close to you—keep me facing your love and your light. When life gets hard; when fear, anger, and sorrow rise; when evil threatens—stir my heart to cry out to you, for I know you will always hear me. You will always guard, defend, and save me. You have made so many good things, but God, nothing is better than you. You are my joy and my refuge. You are my safe place.

Paws in His Presence

God will steady me and hold me through my fears.

The God Who Loves Us

Your unfailing love, O LORD, is as vast as the heavens;
your faithfulness reaches beyond the clouds.
Your righteousness is like the mighty mountains,
your justice like the ocean depths.
You care for people and animals alike, O LORD.
How precious is your unfailing love, O God!
All humanity finds shelter
in the shadow of your wings.
You feed them from the abundance of your own house,
letting them drink from your river of delights.
For you are the fountain of life,
the light by which we see.

PSALM 36:5-9

Paws

Carol wasn't planning to buy a betta fish from the pet store. She had gone there to buy a new brush for her six-year-old cat, Persephone. But when she found an empty rack where the brushes should have been, she went in search of something else. She looked at treats and toys, food and scratching mats, but nothing caught her eye—until she came to an endcap filled with clear plastic cups containing colorful bettas.

Her heart went out to the blue, red, and iridescent–hued fish floating near the bottoms of their tiny cups. For such colorful and fancy-finned fish, they appeared quite melancholy. *I would probably be melancholy, too, if I was stuck in a little cup all day*, Carol reasoned. As she leaned down to look at the next row of fish, she smiled at a tiny dark blue one swimming circles in his cup.

Carol picked up the clear container. The little fish darted to the top of the water, dashed back down, and then resumed his circles. The energetic fish reminded her a little of herself—always moving, always busy.

"Hello, little man. How would you like to live with me?" She looked at the paltry cup. "I'll definitely find you a nicer place to call home."

Having had a betta before, she knew exactly what the little fish would need. She picked out a 2.5 gallon tank, a filter, an overhead light, and a small heater. Then it was time for some interior decorations, with gravel, decorative plants, and a little betta cave to hide in. The small cart was getting full. *Oh, yes. I can't forget the Betta Bites.*

"I promise to take really good care of you," she said as she drove her little fish home.

Persephone was on her cat tower when Carol came in with the fish.

"Sweetie, they didn't have your brush, so I brought you a little brother."

Sephy wasn't very impressed, but Carol suspected she would get more curious once the tank was all set up. And she did. Sephy followed Carol into her home office where the little fish that she had decided to name Howard would stay.

"You are what this room was missing, Howard," Carol said, admiring the navy blue fish in the well-lit tank on her bookshelf.

True to her word, Carol took excellent care of Howard. She cleaned his tank every week, talked to him every day, and made sure anyone who came by the house stopped to admire the handsome fish. As time went by, Howard became so well known among Carol's friends that they often asked about him and occasionally brought him appropriately tiny gifts.

"For such a tiny little man, you sure are loved," Carol would often say.

And he *was* loved.

Carol spent hours watching Howard swim around his tank and dash in and out of his little cave. She even trained him to come up to the surface and bump his nose on her finger when she fed him. Even Persephone warmed up to her aquatic sibling and started napping on a chair near his tank.

As the years went by, Howard slowed down, and he started spending more and more time in his cave—not coming out to play or eat, sometimes for days at a time. And yet Carol's admiration for his contentment with life and his quiet presence only grew stronger.

Even in his stillness, Howard helped her understand a facet of God's love she had never considered before. God's love was not dependent on how productive she was, how busy she stayed, or how well she performed. He simply loved her—perfectly and completely—just as she was.

After all, if she could love a little fish who spent most of his days sleeping contentedly in a cave, how much more did God love her?

"I know you're tired, little man," Carol said to Howard one night before bed. "That's okay. Whatever you need to do is just fine by us." She reached down and scratched Sephy's ears. "Good night, buddy," she said, turning off his little light. "You have no idea how much you are loved."

Carol said the words to Howard—and felt God whisper them back to her.

Ponder

Do you ever feel like you have to earn God's love? What are some things you've done to try to earn his love? Spend a few minutes contemplating God's perfect love—his love that never changes, never runs out, never gives up. His love that sees you—just as you are—and says, "I love you as you are right now." The psalmist says that God cares for people and animals alike. What are some ways God has cared for you recently? How has he cared for the animals in your life?

Pray

God, your love never fails. It is as vast as the heavens, and your faithfulness stretches far beyond the clouds. Your righteousness is like the mighty mountains, and your justice is deeper than the deepest ocean. You are so powerful, and yet you care for us—for the people and animals you have made. How precious is your unfailing love. All humanity can find shelter in the shadow of your wings. You feed us from your hand, from the abundance of your own house. You let us drink from your river of delights. God, you are the fountain of life. You are the light by which we see. Thank you, Lord.

Paws in His Presence

God loves me and he always will.

The God Who Is Trustworthy

O Lord, you alone are my hope.
I've trusted you, O LORD, from childhood.
Yes, you have been with me from birth;
from my mother's womb you have cared for me.
No wonder I am always praising you!
My life is an example to many,
because you have been my strength and protection.
That is why I can never stop praising you;
I declare your glory all day long.

PSALM 71:5-8

Paws

"Ready, Breeze?" Beth asked, trying to suppress her own nerves.

Beth's Golden retriever looked up and gave her one of her trademark big canine smiles. She was the picture of relaxed confidence. Beth's heart swelled with love for the dog she had raised and loved for nearly ten years—one who had birthed three litters of amazing puppies they had been able to share with wonderful families; who was Beth's partner in the sport of agility; and who was so much more than just a dog. She was Beth's best friend.

The two had participated in many competitions before, but this one was different. This would be the last time they would run in the Golden Retriever National. Beth knelt and kissed Breeze's head. She drew in a deep, slow breath to calm herself and focused on the moment.

"We did it, girl," she whispered. "We're here. *You're* here . . ." An involuntary shudder coursed through Beth's body as she thought about all they had been through since their last time at the event.

A year earlier, a tumor had been discovered in Breeze's left eye during a routine veterinary ophthalmologist exam. Beth and her husband were instructed to monitor Breeze for any changes in behavior—and prayed they would find none. However, several months later, the Golden stopped eating and playing. Beth rushed her to the vet's office where they discovered that the tumor had grown and was putting pressure on her eye.

After discussing their limited options, Beth and her husband had made the difficult but necessary decision to remove the affected eye. Since agility was such an important part of Breeze's life—and brought the dog as much joy as it did Beth—quitting the sport had never been an option.

The first time they had walked back into the training facility after surgery, Breeze's tail had swung in happy arcs. But as happy as it made Beth to see her sweet companion back on the course, it quickly became apparent that things were now much harder for her dog. So much of the sport involved Breeze watching Beth for cues and signals. With her left eye gone, Breeze would miss cues from Beth and lose her place on the course.

One particular skill that Breeze had always loved was the dog walk. However, after her surgery, the canine balance beam that had once been so easy for the seasoned champion now seemed like an insurmountable obstacle. But Beth knew her girl could do it, and even more important, she knew Breeze *wanted* to do it.

So Beth and Breeze spent months relearning the skills—and the sport—together. Beth had to learn how to better communicate and work with Breeze from her right side, while Breeze had to learn to navigate the course by keeping her right eye fixed on Beth. It was a slow process, but over time they figured it out.

When Beth saw how excited Breeze was to be back, she had an idea. *What about one more run in the Golden Retriever National?* Breeze's tenth birthday was coming up, and Beth knew her dog wouldn't be able to compete much longer. She would keep doing agility for fun and exercise, but Beth suspected her ribbon-winning dog only had one more event in her. Since the Golden Retriever National was held at Beth's favorite venue—the World Equestrian Center in Florida—with beautiful Golden retrievers filling the space, it seemed like the perfect place for Breeze's final performance.

Now, as Beth took in the audience and the obstacle course they would soon run, she knew she had made the right decision.

"Let's show them what you've got—one last time, girl." Beth said.

A moment later their names were called to take the course.

"Ready, ready! Let's go!" Beth sang out, and the two were off.

They were running a clean and beautiful run. Breeze was hitting every mark, making every move, and completing every jump. There were only two jumps left, and Beth could feel Breeze's excitement. The dog knew she was doing well. So well, in fact, that she turned to look at Beth as if to say, *We're doing it, Mom!* Unfortunately, her momentary glance toward Beth caused her to miss the second-to-last jump. Beth knew the mistake would cost them the title. But it was never about the title. It was about the run.

It was about being there with her girl—her sweet and gentle Breeze.

Beth pulled her dog into a bear hug. "You did it, girl! You were wonderful!"

Tears filled Beth's eyes, tears that fell with abandon when the audience erupted in thunderous applause and gave Breeze a standing ovation. The audience hadn't cared about the missed jump either. All they saw was a champion.

"They are cheering for you, girl," Beth cried into Breeze's fur.

"My hero. My Breeze."

Ponder

What role did faith and trust play in Breeze's ability to run an agility course? In what ways might Breeze's running the agility course serve as a metaphor for someone's faith journey? From the story, how do the words "It was never about the title. It was about the run. It was about being there with her girl" relate to our relationship with God? Psalm 71:7 says, "My life is an example to many, because you have been my strength and protection." In what ways has God shown himself to be your strength and protection?

PRAY

O Lord, you alone are my hope. I have trusted you since childhood. Yes, you have been with me from birth; from my mother's womb you have cared for me. No wonder I am always praising you! Let my life be an example to many because you have been my strength and protection. Let me never stop praising you, Lord. Help me to live my life in a way that brings you glory all my days.

Paws in His Presence

God is good; I can trust him.

The God Who Is with Us

I lift up my eyes to the mountains—
where does my help come from?
My help comes from the LORD,
the Maker of heaven and earth.
He will not let your foot slip—
he who watches over you will not slumber;
indeed, he who watches over Israel
will neither slumber nor sleep.

PSALM 121:1-4, NIV

Paws

Liz stood in the round pen with her favorite horse and sighed. Her shoulders slumped.

Great, she thought, *Duke can't even help.*

An avid horse-lover, Liz loved spending time with Duke. She loved riding him, feeding him, grooming him, and talking to him. Normally, just being present with Duke was enough to quiet the constant loop of negative self-talk that plagued her.

But not today.

Today the hurtful taunts and cruel accusations in her head only grew in volume.

You can't do anything right.

You're never going to succeed at anything.

God doesn't even care enough to answer your prayers and help you.

The last thought hurt worst of all.

It wasn't like she hadn't asked God to quiet her negative thoughts. She begged him every day. She went to church every Sunday, hoping to have a life-changing encounter with God that would free her from her painful self-talk. She had tried breathing techniques and journaling. She wrote positive affirmations on her bathroom mirror and listened to upbeat music, but nothing seemed to work.

"You're just too sensitive," friends would say.

She didn't doubt she was, but she certainly didn't know how to turn off her sensitivity. And even if she could, would she really want to? She just wanted to learn how to better manage and care for her sensitive heart.

"Oh, Duke," she lamented, "why does life have to be so hard? Why does my own brain have to turn on me? And why won't God help me?"

Duke flicked his tail to shoo a pesky horsefly.

Liz sprayed the horse's legs with fly spray, then prepared to clean his hooves. The gentle horse was the epitome of an easygoing animal—except when it came to his feet. Liz always had to work hard to get Duke to lift his hooves so she could clean them. But today, despite her best efforts, the dark bay horse refused to cooperate.

Liz knew she needed to stay calm. She knew her stress would only transfer to the horse. But as Duke continued to keep his feet rooted to the ground instead of offering them to her when she gently squeezed the lower part of his legs, frustration and hurt began to bubble up in her.

"The pasture is muddy, Duke," Liz vented. "We have to clean all that off your hooves, so you don't get another infection. Come on. Help me out, will ya?"

She tried again. The horse refused.

Angry tears spilled from Liz's eyes. *Why won't he listen? Why can't I get him to do this one simple thing?*

Liz dropped the hoof pick in the grooming bucket and went to sit on the mounting block. She covered her face with her hands as a tidal wave of emotion that she had been holding back for weeks came rushing out.

She hated to cry, yet it was the release her heart needed.

Her tears brought with them a flood of painful memories—comments she had pretended hadn't hurt, embarrassing moments she had tried to ignore, people who broke her trust.

"God, it hurts," she muttered into her palms. Then in desperation Liz cried out, "Where are you?"

She felt a gentle nudge as Duke rested his chin against her shoulder.

"Hi, buddy," she whimpered, instantly forgiving him. "Today is on me, not you."

The large horse sighed and kept his chin pressed against her shoulder.

A sudden feeling of peace—one like Liz had never known—washed over her. Her tears stilled. Her heart rate slowed. Her mind grew quiet—blissfully, beautifully quiet.

"God?" Liz whispered in awe. "Is that you?"

She had been praying for a divine encounter, thinking it would happen at church while beautiful music played and devout Christians prayed.

But instead, God chose to meet her in a round pen.

The God of peace found her in the mud and the muck—with a stubborn, wonderful horse resting his chin on her back.

Liz sat up and stroked Duke's side. As she did, she pictured Jesus gently cleaning her weary heart of every hurt and shame-filled memory, just like she had wanted to clean Duke's hooves of the mud and muck. Liz smiled as the feeling of peace continued to grow. Her boots were covered in mud, but she had never felt cleaner or lighter.

Liz suspected she would always struggle with negative self-talk and spiraling thoughts, but in that moment, wrapped in peace, she realized that God hadn't forgotten her. He was with her, and that promise meant she could face anything—even cleaning Duke's hooves.

Ponder

Have you ever had an encounter with God like Liz had in the round pen? If so, spend a few minutes reflecting on that. If not, spend a few minutes asking God to make you aware of his presence with you. Can you relate to Liz's struggle with negative self-talk and spiraling thoughts? How have you dealt with those in the past? How might you deal with them in the future? Have you experienced God cleaning your heart of shame and hurt? Is there anything you need to lay before him today? If so, linger with him a little longer. Let him tend your heart and wrap you in his presence.

PRAY

Lord, I need help. I need the help that only you—the Maker of heaven and earth—can give. Lift my eyes, my heart, and my mind that I might see you. Let my soul remember that you are with me. Remind my heart that you will not let me go. God, I trust you to lead me and guide me and watch over me because I know that you will never slumber or fall asleep on the job. You are with me, and you are for me—that is where my help comes from.

Paws in His Presence

The Maker of heaven and earth loves me and will help me.

Acknowledgments

THIS BOOK WOULD NOT EXIST without the help of some very special people. Especially those who shared their stories with me. I am so grateful to each and every one of you and your precious animals. I pray this book honors your animals and makes you smile.

A huge thank-you to the best publishing team in the entire world: Sarah, Carol, Bonne, Michelle, Dean, Eva, Meg, Brianna, Annette, Natalie, Babs, Jordan, Mark, Glen, and Cheryl! Thank you for being such great partners—and such kind, talented, and amazing people! I am so grateful for each and every one of you.

To my agent, Dave Schroeder, I'm so thankful to have you in my corner—and for all the animal GIFs, puns, and reels you send!

A special thank-you to Brooklyn Stephens at Arise Ranch for creating such a sacred, beautiful, and healing place. You radiate the love and tender care of Jesus, and you are doing good work, my friend.

To PD, sweet, precious PD—thank you for loving my girl. Thank you for being her safe place and for allowing her to encounter God's presence through you. You are more than just a horse—you are her best friend.

To Slick—thank you for walking over to me that horrible, beautiful day. You walked toward my pain, and in doing so, you showed me the love and heart of Jesus.

And to all the barn kitties—thank you for sitting with me—and on me—while I wrote.

Sherri Ferguson, you know I don't normally like getting my picture taken, and yet, you somehow make it fun! Thank you for that beautiful day at Arise!

A big thank-you to my precious friends and family who help me pause and ponder God's presence and goodness on a regular basis—I am so grateful for each one of you. A special thank-you to Jodi G, Aimee, Julie, Barbara, Jodi S, Tracy, and Nicole for letting me talk about book stuff—and for letting me *not* talk about book stuff! Your friendship means a great deal to me.

To Goat-Face and Speed Reader—thank you for one of the best days (and memories) of my life. You are two of God's greatest gifts in my life—you and your Windex that rides at dawn.

Mom, Daddy, Aunt Judy, Aunt Linda, and Mom Bleakley—thank you for being you and for being such an amazing support and prayer team. I am so grateful for you all.

Darrell, Andrew, and Ella—you are my heart and my home. Thank you for believing in me, and in each other, and for always being my safe place. I love you all—and I really, really like you too!

And finally, to my precious Savior and Lord—thank you for meeting me in the mud and the muck of life. Thank you for holding me steady when the world shifts beneath me. Thank you for creating so many precious animals. And thank you for rescuing me with your presence.

About the Author

JENNIFER MARSHALL BLEAKLEY is also the author of *Joey*, the Pawverbs devotional series, *Project Solomon*, and *Finding Grace*. Jen has a master's degree in counseling and worked as a grief counselor for several years before staying home with her children. Somewhere in between countless loads of laundry, library story time, petting zoos, and the blessed hours of nap time, Jen discovered a way to combine her lifelong love of animals and her longing to encourage others with her passion for writing. Jen often says that animals have much to teach us about ourselves, about each other, and about God, but in order to learn from them we must paws and pay attention. (She also really loves a good pun!) Jen lives in Raleigh, North Carolina, with her husband, Darrell; their two children, Andrew and Ella; and a menagerie of pets, including a rescue cat, a sloth-like bearded dragon, and a very needy Golden retriever. You can connect with Jen online at jenniferbleakley.com or on social media @jenbleakley.

Image Credits

Unless otherwise noted, the cover and interior photographs and illustrations are from Unsplash and are the property of their respective copyright holders, and all rights are reserved.

vi Jennifer Marshall Bleakley with her dog, Gracie © GreenFlash Pro Photography

4 Basset hound © ksuksa/Adobe Stock

8 Black kitten meowing © The Lucky Neko

12 Labradoodle © Sander Traa

17 Cat peering from underneath blanket © Mikhail Vasilyev

18 Black horse with bridle © Janosch Diggelmann

22 Bernese mountain dog © Dagmar Klauzová

26 Pictus catfish in aquarium © Robert/ Adobe Stock

30 Jack Russell terrier jumping up © Duncan Kidd

34 Newborn puppy sleeping© Marie Blanton

38 Brown rabbit in the grass © Gary Bendig

42 Tricolor beagle napping © Mina Sh

46 Baby goats playing © Rita Kochmarjova/ Adobe Stock

50 Gray cat with green eyes © Georgiana Voiculescu

54 Pensive older hound © Camilo Castillo

58 Smiling dog sitting in shallow water © Manoj Dharmarathne

63 Golden retriever drenched from swim © Elisa Kennemer

64 Green iguana © John Cobb

68 Yellow Labrador retriever © Natalie Scott

71 Small white dog © Mazlin Massey

72 Dalmatian wearing cone collar © Yulia/ Adobe Stock

76 Black-and-white pony grazing © varbenov/ Adobe Stock

80 Ruby the bird dog © Karen Swallow Prior

84 Bluebird landing on fence © Patrice Bouchard

88 Siberian cat with blue eyes © Massimo Cattaneo/Adobe Stock

92 Dolphins swimming © Arielle Allouche

96 Orange kitten wrapped in towel © Michael Glazier

100 Dog enjoying a head scratch © Ana BG/ Adobe Stock

104 Ruby-throated hummingbird © Keith Martin

108 Pug on couch pillows © Sarandy Westfall

112 Australian heeler © Olga Ovcharenko/ Adobe Stock

116 Barn owl on log © Gilles DETOT

120 Black-and-white terrier © Francesco Ungaro

125 White rabbit in forest © Satyabratasm

126 Black cat lounging on blanket © Ben Moll

131 Orange cat with attentive look © Amber Kipp

132 Young black-and-brown dog © Jessie Shaw

136 Nanny goat with her kid © Serenity Mitchell

140 Hungarian pointer © tmart_foto/Adobe Stock

145 Two dogs running © Alvan Nee

146 Brown horse with white blaze © Callum Hill

151 Brown horse with black mane © Manuel T

152 Cat looking out window © Laura Seidlitz

156 Happy bulldog © Matt Odell

More Great Books by Jennifer Marshall Bleakley

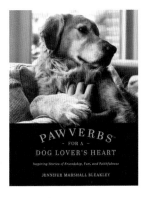

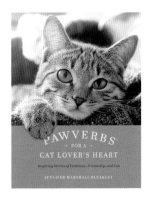

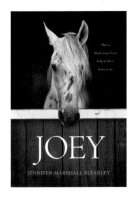

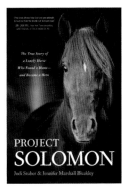

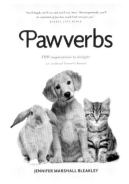

Available everywhere books are sold.